THE MYSTERY
OF THE
LORD'S SUPPER

*Sermons on the Sacrament preached in the
Kirk of Edinburgh
by Robert Bruce in A.D. 1589*

Translated and edited by

THOMAS F. TORRANCE

**RUTHERFORD HOUSE
CHRISTIAN FOCUS**

ISBN 1-84550-056-3

© THOMAS F. TORRANCE 1958
First edition published 1958
Second edition published in 2005
in the
Christian Heritage Imprint
By
Christian Focus Publications, Ltd.,
Geanies House, Fearn, Tain,
Ross-shire, IV20 1TW, Scotland
www.christianfocus.com
and
Rutherford House,
17 Claremont Park, Edinburgh, EH6 7PJ, Scotland
www.rutherfordhouse.org.uk

10 9 8 7 6 5 4 3 2 1

British Library Cataloguing in Publication Data
A catalogue record for this book is available
from The British Library

The right of Thomas F. Torrance to be identified as
Author of this Work has been asserted by him in accordance
with the Copyright, Designs and Patents Act 1988.

Typeset by David Searle, Edinburgh
Cover Design by Alister MacInnes

Printed and bound by Nørhaven Paperback A/S, Denmark

All rights reserved. No part of this publication may be reproduced, stored
in a retrieval system, or transmitted, in any form, by any means, electronic,
mechanical, photocopying, recording or otherwise without the prior
permission of the publisher or a license permitting restricted copying. In
the U.K. such licenses are issued by the Copyright Licensing Agency, 90
Tottenham Court Road, London, W1P 9HE.

CONTENTS

Five Sermons

PREFACE

to the first edition (1958)

FROM early years the historic *Sermons of Robert Bruce on the Sacrament* formed an essential and unforgettable part of my theological diet. I was brought up on them at home, and when I came to New College, in the University of Edinburgh, as a divinity student, I found myself giving them fuller study on the urgent recommendation of Professor H. R. Mackintosh. His own lectures on the Sacraments which drew so much inspiration from Bruce's sermons taught me to treasure them even more highly as the very marrow of our sacramental tradition in the Church of Scotland. Ever since they were first delivered in the Great Kirk of St. Giles, Edinburgh, in February and March, 1589, their doctrine has passed into the soul of the Kirk, building up its faith and informing its worship at the Table of the Lord, in spite of the fact that comparatively few editions of the Sermons have actually been published for three hundred years

The original edition of the Sermons was published in 1590 and 1591 with a dedicatory epistle to James the sixth, King of Scots, which I have left in their original form in order to give the reader some indication of the Scots tongue as used by Bruce. The Sermons were taken down as they were received from Bruce's mouth and published without any rewriting or polishing. To read them in the rich language and force of their delivery enables one to appreciate the comment of John Livingstone, a younger contemporary: 'Master Robert

Bruce I heard several times, and, in my opinion, never man spake with greater power since the Apostles' days.'

In 1614 the little book of Sermons was 'taught to speak English', as it was put, and published in London under the title of *The Mystery of the Lord's Supper*. Three years later the same translation, apparently by one M. S. Mitchell, was revised and reissued along with the other eleven sermons published first in 1591, also done into English, under the title: *'The Way to true Peace and Rest*, delivered at Edinborough in Sixteen Sermons on the Lord's Supper, Hezekiah's Sickness, and other select Scriptures, by that reverend and faithful Preacher of God's Word, Mr. Robert Bruce, for the present Minister of the Word in Scotland.'

The Scots text of all these sermons was republished by William Cunningham in Edinburgh in 1843, along with a life of Bruce by Wodrow, and a number of relevant documents and letters by Bruce and others. Another English translation of the first five sermons on the Sacrament only, still preserving something of the quaintness of the original, was published in 1901 by H. R. Mackintosh's predecessor, Professor John Laidlaw, together with a biographical sketch based on that of Wodrow.

It is now my privilege as successor to Cunningham, Laidlaw, and Mackintosh, in New College, in offering a new translation of these sermons, to pass on this treasure from our Scottish heritage to another generation, under the title of the 1614 edition. I am aware that publication in this more modern form does not do justice to the vigour and power of the old Scots speech, but it is my hope that it will enable Bruce's work to be read and appreciated more widely than ever before. Scholars will want to turn to the original text.

This edition is not for them but for the general membership in the Kirk, the successors of those to whom the sermons were first delivered. While trying to keep as close as possible to the original text, and to preserve Bruce's striking style, I have taken the liberty of rearranging clauses and sentences again and again in order to bring out more clearly the logic of the argument, and frequently also of shortening them when the exposition seemed needlessly repetitious, at least according to modern standards. The citations from the Scriptures which Bruce took as a rule from the Geneva Bible I have given according to our familiar Authorised and Revised versions.

I should like to acknowledge my great debt to Mrs. E. R. Olbrycht for her patience and care in helping me with the typing.

THOMAS F. TORRANCE

New College
Edinburgh
July, 1957

PREFACE

to the 2005 edition

I AM deeply grateful to Professor T. F. Torrance for his gracious permission for Rutherford House to reprint this major work of Robert Bruce on *The Lord's Supper*. I am also indebted to William Mackenzie of Christian Focus Publications for agreeing to co-publish this volume, thus ensuring as wide a distribution of it as possible. Professor Torrance's translation of the original text, first published in 1590, remains unchanged. However, in addition to two minor footnotes, I have taken the liberty of inserting into the text occasional headings in the hope of helping readers to find their way through some fairly long paragraphs and to facilitate their understanding of Bruce's carefully presented sermons with their profound theological content.

My own second charge in the Church of Scotland was the 'auld Kirk of Larbert' where in 1626 Bruce is thought to have built a new manse—now known as 'the old manse' which still stands today as the oldest inhabited house in Stirlingshire—and where in the same year at his own expense he restored the original church which had fallen into a state of decay. There Bruce preached regularly for six years from 1625 until his death in 1631 and it is hardly surprising that vast crowds travelled to Larbert each Sunday to hear his powerful proclamation of the Word of God.

He was buried at the foot of the pulpit within the building where he had ministered in these latter years of his life, and a great stone was placed horizontally over his grave. However, as the original church building was demolished in 1820 when the present handsome Georgian sanctuary was erected, the gravestone with its challenging inscription—no longer under the Kirk roof but exposed to the elements—was beginning to be seriously eroded. I therefore sought the permission of Lord Elgin, Bruce's direct descendent, to bring the stone into the protection of the new church.

There, just inside the main entrance, it now stands with its challenging inscription: *Cristus vita et in morte lucrum,* 'Christ is life and in death is gain' (cf. Phil. 1:21).[1] Readers of Professor Torrance's Introduction to this book will quickly grasp the relevance of such words.

May this second edition be a significant contribution to the understanding and practice of the 21st Century church of Christ's priceless gift to her of *The Mystery of the Lord's Supper.*

DAVID C SEARLE
Edinburgh, 2005

---

[1] The Latin words are held to be from Beza's version of Philippians 1:21 on which was based the Geneva Version which Bruce himself used; the wording, however, is very slightly different, probably to facilitate the mason's task of carving the stone. His personal copy of the Geneva Bible is still in the possession of Lord Elgin.

INTRODUCTION

Robert Bruce of Kinnaird

ROBERT BRUCE, the successor in St. Giles's, Edinburgh, to James Lawson and John Knox, was one of the most deeply spiritual and powerful ministers of the Gospel Scotland has ever known. Born in the troublous times just before the Reformation, and endowed with singular gifts, he was cast by Providence for a difficult role in the Kingdom of Christ which he fulfilled with such grace and integrity, through bringing the Gospel to the hungry multitudes and through sheer personal worth in the midst of intrigue and bitterness in Church and State, that the Kirk owes him an immeasurable debt. It was largely under his leadership that the Reformation in Scotland was given the stability and permanence which it had not attained even under the leadership of Knox, while the evangelical tradition in Word and Sacrament and in the pastoral care of the flock of Christ was given lasting character through his outstanding ministrations.

Robert Bruce was the second son of Sir Alexander Bruce of Airth Castle, Stirlingshire, one of the ancient barons of Scotland, and claiming descent from the blood royal. His mother, Janet Livingstone, was a great-granddaughter of James I and a staunch Roman Catholic. In 1568 his father, an adherent of the Reformed cause, sent Robert to study the humanities at St. Salvator's College, St. Andrews, when George Buchanan was still Principal of St. Leonard's, Andrew Melville was teaching in St. Mary's and his friend James

Melville came up in 1571 as a fellow-student. In these circumstances Robert Bruce could not but come under the powerful influence of the Reformed teaching, while his last year before he commenced as Master of Arts in 1572 coincided with the last year of John Knox's life, which he spent in St. Andrews in preaching and teaching. Like John Calvin, Robert Bruce was designed by his father for the civil law, and went from St. Andrews to France and the Low Countries in pursuit of further study, notably at Louvain.

On return from the Continent he took up the practice of law and rapidly acquired a considerable reputation, so that his father had him endowed with the barony of Kinnaird, near Larbert, with a view to his becoming a senator in the College of Justice. But all this time Bruce had been feeling increasingly drawn to the study of divinity by 'a mighty inward working', as he confided to Melville, which allowed him to get no rest and brought him into fearful agony of conscience as he fought against it. It is also apparent that his high sense of justice and integrity recoiled from the kind of life he was being forced to lead as a courtier in Edinburgh, and made him readier to surrender it for the service of the Church. To this course his parents were resolutely opposed, but eventually with the reluctant acquiescence of his father he returned to St. Andrews and began his study for the ministry. But Bruce must be allowed to tell his own story, in an account that dates from 1624 and is preserved for us by Calderwood and Wodrow:

'Concerning my vocation to the ministry, I was first called to grace before I obeyed my calling to the ministry. He made me first a Christian, before He made me a minister. For long I opposed my calling to the

2

ministry. For ten years, at least, I never lept on horseback or alighted, without my conscience opposing and justly accusing me. At last it pleased God, in the year 1581, in the month of August, in the last night of the month, as I lay in the new loft chamber at Airth, to smite me inwardly and judicially in my conscience, and to present all my sins before me in such a way that He omitted no circumstance, but made my conscience see time, place and conscience as vividly as in the hour I committed them. He made the devil accuse me so audibly, that I heard his voice as vividly as ever I heard anything, not being asleep but awake. So far as he spoke the truth my conscience bore him record, and testified against me very clearly, but when he came to be a false accuser and laid things to my charge which I had never done, then my conscience failed him, and refused to testify with him. But in the things that were true my conscience condemned me, and the condemner tormented me, and made me feel the wrath of God pressing me down, as it were, to the bottom of hell. Indeed, I was so fearfully and extremely tormented, that I would have been content to have been cast into a cauldron of hot moulten lead, in order to have my soul relieved of that insupportable weight. Always, as far as he spoke the truth, I confessed and restored God to His glory, and cried to God for His mercy for the merits of Christ. I appealed every time to His mercy, purchased by the blood, death, and passion of Christ. Through the bottomless mercy of God, this court of justice held over my soul turned into a court of mercy for me, for that same night, before ever the day dawned or the sun rose, He restrained those furies and outcries of my justly accusing conscience, and enabled me to arise in the morning.

'There was a brother in the ministry lying beside me that night. I commended my painful state to his prayers, but I found him a comfortless comforter. This visitation was the first thing that chased me to grace. Long before this I had resisted, but after that I resolved to go to St. Andrews to Mr Andrew Melville, and there to tell him my trouble, and to communicate to him all my griefs. It was long before I got leave to go, for my mother put so many impediments in my way. My father at last condescended, but my mother refused, until I resigned some lands and entitlements. And that I did willingly, casting my clothes from me, my vain and glorious apparel, sent my horse to the market, and divested myself of all impediments, and went to the New College. There I abode for long before I dared to open my mouth—I was so bashful and oppressed with shame and blushing. Mr Andrew wanted me to take part in the class-exercises, but I did not dare to begin there. At length I agreed to be heard privately, and went to a room, and asked Mr James Melville, and Mr John Dury, and some of the best men, to hear me, and then I went to take part at the table and finally went to the lecture-room and took my turn in giving the exposition before a large crowd, as there are many still alive to testify.

'At last, in the year 1587, in the month of June, Mr Andrew Melville took me over with him to a General Assembly held in Edinburgh. At that time Edinburgh lacked pastors, and they drew up a leet of names with my name among the others, and gave it to the General Assembly. They insisted that I should take my place among the others in teaching one day before the Assembly. After long entreaty on their part I agreed and gave an exposition about the spiritual armour from the sixth chapter of Ephesians. The Assembly convened in session and was very crowded, I remember. Mr Udal, the Englishman, was there, and various other strangers. At last they came to consider the leet, to decide who was to be appointed. I was chosen and appointed with virtually universal consent, very few being against. Thus the charge was laid upon me severely against my will, for at the same time I had an outward call to St. Andrews, with the consent of the whole University, and all the gentlemen round about. I still have all their subscriptions to testify to that, and certainly I would have preferred to go to St. Andrews; I had no desire for the Court for I knew well that the Court and I could never agree.

Therefore for a long time I refused the brethren in Edinburgh and went over to St. Andrews. I remained there no time at all, for I was sent for at once by the Provost and Council of Edinburgh. James Dalziel, the provost's son-in-law and several others were sent to fetch me. I was loath to go, but they threatened me with authority; so I took counsel with God and thought it right to obey, not fully to take on the charge but only to try it out for a while to see how the Lord would bless my work. I found such a barrier between His Majesty's comfortable presence [i.e. God's presence] and me, that I thought it was not His Majesty's pleasure that I should take the full burden upon me until this barrier was demolished and all hindrance removed. And so in process of time I at length agreed, and remained nearly twelve years in Edinburgh, when I was driven out, and have now been banished for twenty-six years. I was twice in France, once before my calling to the ministry, next when I was a minister because of the Master of Gowrie. I am still not free from fears, and constant attempts to banish me again.

'May the Lord in His infinite mercy grant that I may end my course well, end it with joy, and fight a good fight to keep the faith, to perfect my ministry, with the approval of God in Christ, and of a good conscience. Amen.'

That brief sketch of his life and ministry, dictated by Bruce toward the end of his life, gives us a profound and moving insight into the man who preached these sermons. It will be sufficient for our purpose here to fill in that sketch only at a number of significant points with certain details of considerable interest.

It was several years after his initial call that Bruce was persuaded to accept the charge in Edinburgh permanently, and several years after that that he was formally ordained to the ministry of Word and Sacrament. In extreme reluctance to assume the full burden of office through the imposition of hands by the Presbytery, he kept offering his services in preaching only for restricted periods, although it was pressed upon him year after year by the congregation and the Presbytery. Eventually he was made to yield in altogether exceptional circumstances, of which a vivid account has been left us by John Livingstone:

'One day one of the ministers giving the Communion, desired Mr Robert Bruce, who was to preach in the afternoon, to sit by him; and when he himself had served two or three tables, he went out of the church as if he were shortly to return, but sent in word to Mr Bruce with some of the elders that he would not return at that time. And therefore Mr Robert was obliged to serve the rest of the tables, or else the ministration would come to an end. Therefore when the eyes of the whole people were upon him, and many also cried to him to serve the table now filled, he went on and administered the Communion to the rest, with such singular assistance and elevated affections among the people, as had not been seen in that place before.'

It was of course quite out of order, but once Bruce had been forced to take the elements in his hands, and had celebrated the Sacrament, he felt that, along with the approbation of the ministry and the congregation already fully given, he had 'the material' of ordination, and thereafter discharged in St. Giles the duties of a fully ordained minister. This clearly reflects the Old Testament concept of consecration to priesthood through 'the filling of the hands' with the oblations, which for many centuries was remarkably echoed in the Western Church in the conception that at ordination 'the filling of the hands' was more important than 'the imposition of hands'. Be that as it may, the omission of formal ordination through the imposition of hands according to the order of the Kirk later became the cause of a serious dispute between Bruce and the King as well as between Bruce and the Presbytery.

The occasion arose in 1598 when at the instance of Bruce himself among others the town was being divided into eight parishes with eight ministers who could then adequately discharge their pastoral office each with a particular congregation. When Bruce consented to take charge of a particular flock, the King insisted that he should now be formally ordained. Bruce insisted that while he was ready to receive 'the imposition of hands' in being admitted to a particular charge, he could not submit to a '*new* ordination' which would call in question the ministry which God had blessed so evidently for eight or nine years. 'The imposition of hands' would have to be interpreted in this case as an act of 'confirmation' of the ministry he had hitherto given in Word and Sacrament. The Presbytery was deeply sympathetic with Bruce, but eventually after prolonged discussion in which it became clear to Bruce that all his trusted brethren regarded his former 'ordination' as irregular, he agreed to receive 'the imposition of hands' and was formally inducted into his charge. According to Wodrow, this is the only instance of irregularity of its kind known in the Church.

His famous *Sermons on the Sacrament* were delivered in St. Giles in 1589, nine years earlier, presumably after he had been induced to administer the Sacrament himself. Although we cannot but agree with the Presbytery in its insistence that Bruce had to receive 'ordinary ordination', it must be acknowledged without any hesitation that his ministry of Word and Sacrament from the beginning had been blessed in an unparalleled way with the mighty efficacy of the Spirit. The congregation found it extremely difficult to understand why their minister had thus to be ordained, and Bruce who had a pastor's heart, if ever any man had, was deeply aware of the offence it might cause to his flock, especially to the poor and simple folk. But in point of fact his ministry went on from strength to strength, and God did not suffer anything that he had hitherto done to fall to the ground. As Melville put it in his diary: 'The godly for his potent and moving doctrine loved him; the worldly for his parentage and position reverenced him; and the enemies for both reasons stood in awe of him.' Similar is the account of Robert Fleming: 'Whilst he was in the ministry of Edinburgh he shone as a great light through the whole land, the power and efficacy of the Spirit most sensibly accompanying the Word he preached. He was a terror to evil-doers, and the authority of God did so appear in him and his carriage, with such a majesty in his countenance, that it compelled fear and respect from the greatest in the land, even from those who were avowed enemies of godliness. Indeed, it was known what awful impressions King James himself had of him; and once he even gave the testimony before many, that he judged Mr Bruce was worth the half of his kingdom.'

A little earlier than this Bruce married Martha Douglas of Parkhead who proved to be a very brave and loyal companion to her husband in his troubled life. Bruce's father, Sir Alexander Bruce of Airth, restored to him at this time the estate of Kinnaird which provided him, and his family, with a place of security and retreat from the exacting life in the service of the Kirk. Two daughters and two sons were born to the Bruces. One of the sons who later succeeded his father as the Laird of Kinnaird was attached to the court, while the other, like the two sons of John Knox, became a minister of the Church of England. We do not know much of Bruce's domestic life, but, judging from the hints and flashes of autobiographical insight in the sermons and letters, his home must have been a veritable house of God, and a constant refuge for the troubled in spirit. In Edinburgh he lived in a house immediately opposite the Kirk of St. Giles.

During this early period of his ministry Bruce was twice Moderator of the General Assembly. A special meeting of the Assembly had been convened in February, 1588, under the threat of invasion through the

Spanish Armada. To everybody Bruce was clearly the man to match the hour; such was his reputation for wisdom and management, that he was elected Moderator with acclaim on all sides. The vigour and power with which he handled the situation and the firmness of his measures against the corrupt popery of those days left a profound impression on both Church and State. It was apparent to all that God had raised up a man fit to stand in the shoes of John Knox and like him to put spirit and courage into the whole nation. The sermons he preached from Psalm 76 on the two Sundays following the defeat of the Spanish Armada are outstanding examples of his power to proclaim the Word of God to the nation.

It was no doubt due to the impression Bruce made as Moderator of the Assembly and minister of St. Giles, bearing no small part of the burden of the public affairs of the Kirk, and proving helpful to the King and his Chancellor by his wise advice, that led the King to entrust the affairs of State largely to the wisdom and care of Bruce when in November of 1598 he left the country for Norway to bring home his bride, Princess Anne of Denmark. For six months Bruce was virtually regent of the country, though he never exercised any formal office of State, and it was largely owing to his guidance and grasp of affairs that the country kept perfectly calm and peaceful. The letters from King James and Sir John Maitland, the Chancellor, to Bruce during these months show the highest regard and esteem for his services, the King in particular acknowledging to Bruce that 'he was worthy of the quarter of his *petite* kingdom'. On the return of the royal couple it fell to Bruce to anoint the Queen at her Coronation in the Abbey Church, which he did with 'a bonnie quantity of oil', after three sermons in Latin, French, and English had been preached, and two short discourses by Bruce and Craig were made to the poor woman!

The second occasion on which Bruce was elected Moderator of the Assembly was in 1592, a year outstanding in the history of the Church of Scotland for the Assembly's vigorous acts regarding the discipline and patrimony of the Kirk, and for the act of Parliament, meeting immediately after the Assembly, which finally established the polity of the Kirk and ratified the liberty of Assemblies, Synods and Presbyteries. The triumph of the Reformation was thus firmly secured. It is not surprising, then, that these acts legalising the principles of the Second Book of Discipline have come to be regarded as the great charter of Scottish Presbyterianism.

Meantime friction between the Church and the King had been growing steadily. The King was determined to gain control over the affairs of the Church and had embarked upon a policy of gradual attrition. He objected to the fact that the reformed bishops or superintendents established under Knox were subject to the authority of Presbyteries and provincial Synods as well as the General Assembly, and began to intrude on his own another kind of bishop upon the Church invested with, and therefore subject to, the authority of the State. At the same time in order to strengthen his hands over against the Kirk he began to cultivate the friendship of the Catholic lords, and so to be unjustly lenient with their subversive activity especially against the establishment of the reformed ministry throughout the parishes of the land. This was aggravated by the failure of the King to take adequate measures in support of colleges and schools and in the provision of ministers, and adequate measures against wide-spread corruption, injustice and violence, and the increase of poverty. Matters began to come to a head with the murder of the Earl of Moray, a staunch adherent of the Reformed Kirk, by the Earl of Huntly, a notorious Catholic favoured by the King. When the Kirk placed Huntly under the ban of excommunication, the King was enraged and threatened to break the heads of the ministers, and though he sought to recover some support from them by having Parliament ratify the acts of Assembly that same year, 1592, he was all the more determined to bring the Kirk to heel.

Robert Bruce himself, who had hitherto enjoyed the full favour of the King, was now brought directly into the quarrel between the King and the Church when a base and groundless charge was brought against him of giving refuge with treacherous intent to the wild Earl of Bothwell, who had recently tried to take the King's life. Whereupon the King attacked the loyalty of the ministers, accusing them of denouncing others as traitors when they were shielding one themselves, and the main bitterness of his attack fell upon Bruce. As soon as the treasonable charge against him was shown to be false, the King tried to brush it aside and have the whole issue hushed up, but Bruce was adamant and insisted that his name be absolutely cleared. It was not only, he felt, that his own honour was at stake, but the honour of his calling in the ministry. What Bruce demanded was apparently too much for the King's pride, with the result that his deep injury to Bruce, and his consciousness of it, led to a bitter estrangement which the King, already jealous of Bruce's popularity, deliberately fostered in order at last in 1600 to have Bruce banished from the pulpit of St. Giles and from his dominant influence in the General Assembly.

That year there took place a perplexing incident in Perth on a visit of the King to the Earl of Gowrie who had recently returned from the Continent an ardent supporter of the Reformed Church. According to the King, the Earl of Gowrie and his brother attempted to kill him, but were themselves slain. Many found it difficult to believe that this was a true version of what happened, for years of intrigue and unpopularity had contributed to destroy confidence in the King's word. Bruce found it particularly difficult to make up his mind about it, and declined to proclaim from the pulpit the King's version of the affair. This in turn did an injury to the honour of the King, and though Bruce became more and more convinced that Gowrie had actually conspired against his majesty's person, and signed a document to that effect to help clear the name of the King, he still refused to declaim about it from the pulpit where he was called only to proclaim the Word of God. In preaching he was the ambassador of Christ, and took his instructions and commission from Him and not from another. No earthly prince, he argued, had power to give instructions to another Prince's ambassador. The reaction of the King was to suspend Bruce from preaching, to remove him from Edinburgh, and then to banish him to France. The following year, however, he was allowed to return, on the intercession of the Earl of Mar, but was 'warded' in his own house at Kinnaird.

During the next two years before his accession to the throne of England, James managed to get most of the leading ministers who remained to resist his will either silenced or banished. Then in 1605 he persuaded the Assembly to have Bruce 'removed' from his office as minister of Edinburgh, and banished him to Inverness to be 'warded' there. In spite of considerable opposition and personal annoyance, Bruce remained with his family there for eight years, exercising a wonderful ministry that extended its influence all over the north. People came incredible distances to hear his preaching. At last the Highlands really had the Gospel preached to them and 'many were converted, and multitudes edified'.

According to the early account given by Robert Fleming, 'When Bruce was confined at Inverness, that poor dark country was marvellously enlightened, many were brought into Christ by his ministry, and a seed sown in these places, which to this day is not worn out.'

A change was in store for Bruce in 1613 when, through the influence of his son Robert at the Court in England, he was allowed to return to Kinnaird. There he built up at his own expense the ruined church of Larbert and ministered the Word and Sacrament. Though nominally confined to his house, he travelled much over central Scotland preaching the Gospel and visiting ministers, and was found as far afield as Ayr, Cramond, and Leuchars. His reputation as a man of God, as an expositor and teacher of the Word, and as a pastor with marvellous insight into the troubles of the soul, was so great that people came in great numbers from far and near to visit him at Kinnaird, much to the distress of his enemies, so that grounds for a charge against Bruce were eagerly seized when he was found making a secret visit to Edinburgh in 1621 on a purely domestic purpose that required his personal attendance. His faithful wife, who had undertaken such errands for him, had recently died, and he was forced to undertake them himself. For this offence he was shut up in the Castle, pending the pleasure of the King. James sent word that he was to be banished once more to Inverness, and when it was decided in Edinburgh that he might be allowed to spend the winter at Kinnaird, the King wrote again blaming those responsible for the delay, alleging that 'it was not for love of Mr Robert, but to keep up the schism in the Kirk', and insisted that 'he should not allow any more popish pilgrimages to Kinnaird'!

By this time James had succeeded in intruding his Erastian form of episcopacy upon the Church, and it is not to be wondered at that the popularity and influence of Bruce brought upon him the jealousy and petty persecution of the King's men in the Church. They sent their agents to spy out his activities, informed against him at Court, and eventually procured his banishment once again to Inverness in 1622. There he took up again his ministry with as great success as ever, but after two years was allowed to return to Kinnaird to attend to his domestic affairs. Shortly afterwards the King died, and Bruce was not forced to return to the north. There he lived for the rest of his days, travelling round the countryside as before, but now perhaps his chief ministry was that of a veritable 'father in God' to many of the younger ministers, who came to sit at his feet and to learn from his deeply spiritual and prayerful devotion to his Lord. One of them wrote of him:

'No man in his time spoke with such evidence and power of the Spirit. No man had so many seals of conversion, indeed many of his hearers thought no man,

since the Apostles, spoke with such power. He had a
notable faculty of searching deeply into the Scriptures,
and making the darkest mysteries very plain, but
especially in dealing with people's consciences. He was
much exercised in conscience himself, both in public
and in private. He was very short in prayer when others
were present, but every sentence was like a strong bolt
up to heaven. I have heard him say that he wearied
when others were long in prayer, but when alone he
spent much time in wrestling and in prayer.'

During the last two or three years of his life his public
appearances were apparently but few, but one of them
deserves to be noted: his visit to the Kirk of Shotts in
June, 1630, to take part in Communion services to
which many people resorted from different parts of the
country. They lasted four or five days, but it is mostly
for the preaching of John Livingstone, one of Bruce's
young friends, that the occasion is remembered—the
sermon on Ezekiel 36:25-6: 'Then will I sprinkle clean
waters upon you, and ye shall be clean: a new heart also
will I give you, and a new spirit will I put within you.' It
was an occasion of the greatest blessing and of an
extraordinary movement of the Spirit among all who
were present, the inspiration of which lasted long into
the days of the Covenanters.

When John Knox lay dying he asked his wife to read
to him 'where he first cast his anchor', the seventeenth
chapter of John's Gospel. When the call came for Robert
Bruce it was to the eighth chapter of Romans that he
turned. A little after breakfast on the twenty-seventh of
July, 1631, he told his daughter Martha that his Master
was calling him. He asked for the Bible, but, finding
that he was unable to read, he said, 'Turn me up the

eighth chapter of Romans, thirty-eighth verse': 'For I am persuaded that neither life nor death shall be able to separate me from the love of God which is in Christ Jesus my Lord.' Then, putting his finger on the words in front of him, he said, 'God be with you my children. I have breakfasted with you, and shall sup with my Lord Jesus Christ this night,' and immediately gave up his spirit to God. 'Thus', says Wodrow, 'this great champion for the truth, and the crown and interest of his Master, who knew not what it was to be afraid of the face of man, was taken off the field as more than a conqueror, and had an abundant entrance into the everlasting Kingdom of his Lord and Saviour.' He was buried at the foot of the pulpit in the Church at Larbert which he himself had restored from pre-Reformation ruins and where he had frequently preached in his final few years, but his teaching is for ever embedded in the heart of the Kirk he loved and did so much to reform and raise up to the glory of God.

Few men in the history of the Kirk can stand beside Bruce in sheer godliness and absolute fidelity to conviction. The resolute uprightness, the righteous tenacity in which he lived his life from beginning to end, was in itself a supreme contribution to the nation. His example as a true minister of Word and Sacrament, and as a faithful and tender pastor with his flock at all times and in spite of every difficulty and rebuff, taught and inspired not only those who followed him immediately in the ministry, but thousands of others since who have been called into the holy office of the Gospel in Scotland. Even greater has been the impact of his teaching in which Bruce applied the high doctrines of the Reformed Church directly to the personal conscience. No Scottish divine, to my knowledge, had more of Calvin's supreme sense of the Majesty and Mercy of God, but in the piety of Bruce emphasis is laid upon the *feeling* of that Majesty and Mercy in a way that it is not in Calvin. Bruce is far closer to the theology and biblical outlook of Calvin than the Westminster divines of the next generation, but already in Bruce there is a shift of emphasis clearly evident in the focus of so much attention upon *conscience*. That comes out not only in the demand for strict self-examination on the part of minister and congregation alike, but in the concept of conscious 'access' through a repentant and prayerful spirit to the presence and power of God.

All this carried with it a number of significant implications, three of which may be noted:

(*a*) The alliance of high doctrine to the response of the heart laid the inundation for that integration between doctrinal teaching and personal application, between sacramental ministration and evangelical quickening so characteristic of the Scottish tradition. That was certainly one of the outstanding marks of the ministry of Bruce's friends and colleagues such as Craig, Davidson, Pont, Simpson, and Livingstone. It was above all at the Sacrament of the Lord's Supper that this was apparent, for the Sacrament was not only the supreme ordinance of prayer and worship and of feeding upon Christ, but emphatically an evangelical ordinance through which the Gospel was proclaimed in the most vivid and potent way and through which multitudes were brought into Christ and sealed by the Spirit. In the language of a later day, the Sacrament was also a 'converting ordinance', for it was at the Sacrament, before the gracious presence of the divine Majesty, that sinners were convicted of sin and converted to godliness. This combination of sacramental and evangelical experience secured the latter from subjectivist pietism, and the former from a doctrinaire sacramentalism. But where in this development the emphasis tended to fall upon the conscience rather than upon the Word of the Gospel, upon self-examination rather than thankfulness and praise to God, the ground was laid for that reproachful self-questioning of faith, and almost morbid fear of the Majesty of God and His requirements in the Sacrament, which are still marked characteristics of Scottish piety in parts of the Highlands.

(b) In his own case, the emphasis upon inward feeling of the Majesty and Mercy of God, laid Bruce open to the temptations of doubt that sometimes assailed Luther, but never Calvin or Knox. To cite Robert Fleming once again: 'He was a man that had much inward exercise about his own personal case, and had been oft assaulted anent that great foundation truth, the being of a God, which cost him many days and nights wrestling. When he came up to the pulpit, after he had been silent a little, as was his usual way, he would sometimes say, "I think it's a great matter to believe that there is a God"; telling the people it was another thing to believe than what they judged.' In Bruce this tendency to be afflicted with seasons of doubt was not due to a naturally sceptical mind but rather to a serious wrestling with the problems of conscience, and it was always correlative to his evangelical experience. It was this that helped Bruce to understand so deeply the fearfulness of those hounded by their conscience, and helped him to preach as no other on the pacification of the conscience in the mercy of God. But once such a conscience is cut adrift from the evangelical message and moralised, as it tended to be through the exaggerated moralism of the Larger

Catechism, it could lead only too easily into the moral and philosophic doubt that have so often characterised Scottish Universities, not always excepting their theologians.

(c) Once again, in Bruce's own case, the amazing sense of the divine Majesty, together with his scrupulous culture of an upright conscience, tended to breed an unduly punctilious sense of honour. Here Bruce's greatness was also the occasion of his weakness, as even M'Crie admitted in 'granting that he gave way to scrupulosity, that he required a degree of evidence as to the guilt of Gowrie, which was not necessary to justify the part he was to take in announcing it, that there was a mixture of pride in his motives and that he stood too much on the point of honour'. It is difficult to resist the conclusion that if Bruce had stood less upon the claims of offended honour before the King and had harnessed his conscience less to the complete satisfaction of his own scruples, he would have maintained throughout a powerful influence upon the King, and would have remained in Edinburgh to guide the whole course of the Church and the Gospel through a very difficult period. As it was, the stubborn, almost unreasonable, conscience of Bruce contributed unnecessarily and doubtless fatally to the tension between Church and King. He was, of course, not alone in that, and certainly not the most outspoken of the ministers in remonstrance with the King, but as the principal Minister of Edinburgh he occupied a position of the greatest responsibility in relation to the King and Court, and could not but draw upon himself the full opposition of the King if he resisted him. Certainly the treatment meted out to Bruce was scandalous and disgraceful, but much of that might never have arisen had he had a wider sympathy and a greater respect for the conscience of others even when it might contradict the scruples of his own. He tended to live too much by the private judgements of his own conscience and not enough by the sheer Word of the Gospel, forgetting, perhaps, that if our heart condemns us, God is greater than our heart, infinitely greater. That is the Majesty of His Mercy. Over against that the Christian conscience is not something that a man possesses in himself, but something that he shares with his fellow-believers, and above all that which they in togetherness share with God, a *con-science* which is their joint knowing of the Divine will in Christ announced to them through the Gospel. The tendency for the conscience to rely upon itself as an autonomous or semi-autonomous principle was characteristic of the humanism of the Renaissance, and tended in the second and third generations of the Reformation to occupy a large place in Protestantism, notably in English Puritanism. It was in fact a lapse back into Stoic rather than into early Christian virtue. In Calvinism this tendency came back through its strong Augustinianism so apparent in Bruce, though here too doubtless it owed something to the outlook fostered by the classical studies of George Buchanan and Andrew Melville in St. Andrews. In Robert Bruce it was allied to an uncommonly deep spiritual nature, and certainly contributed greatly to his understanding of repentance, though it often made him desperately uneasy and hungry for absolute assurance which he found above all in the Sacrament of the Lord's Supper.

If the indomitable conscience of Bruce was also evidence of a weakness which he had in common with so many of his generation, it nevertheless remains true that he stands out amongst them all as a supremely great and saintly man with unswerving fidelity to His Master and ungrudging faithfulness to his divine calling as a Minister of the Gospel. It is, however, as a theologian above all that we must appreciate him today. He wrote no works of theology, but there can be no doubt from what he has left us that he was a man of commanding theological power and spiritual insight, as also a man of rare faith. Of all men in his generation, except perhaps John Craig, his Calvinist theology was still genuinely that of John Calvin himself, and of the *Scots Confession*, and not that of the 'Calvinism' which was an amalgam of Aristotelian logic and the Reformed faith, which lay behind the Synod of Dort (1618), and through it came to be regarded as 'classical Calvinism'. Moreover, though Bruce was apparently acquainted with the works of the greatest of all Protestant Scholastic theologians, Amandus Polanus of Basel, there is no trace of that academic scholasticism in his own theology. Was this by any chance due to the supremely evangelical and pastoral concern of John Knox who wrote from St. Andrews in 1572, in his last letter to the General Assembly, a warning against subjecting the pulpit to the judgement of the schools? 'Above all things', he said, 'preserve the Kirk from the bondage of the Universities'! At any rate, the alliance of theology with preaching and worship, in the great tradition of Knox and Calvin, was a prime characteristic of Robert Bruce. Like Calvin, also, Bruce was steeped in the learning of the Fathers of the Early Church, being particularly influenced by Augustine, and Irenaeus, 'that ancient writer', as Bruce called him. It was probably this combination of Biblical and Patristic theology that kept him so close to Calvin especially at a number of significant points where rationalistic Calvinism lost touch with Calvin himself, owing to its combination of theology with a revived Aristotelianism, and later indeed with Cartesian philosophy, both so markedly evident in the great theologians of the Netherlands who came to occupy a dominant influence over many Scottish divines.

This is not the place to offer an exposition of the theology of Robert Bruce, but one very important matter, related to what has been said above and bearing upon his teaching on the Sacrament of the Lord's Supper, ought to be noted and considered. I refer to the doctrine of *union with Christ* and of *our participation in his saving and sanctifying humanity*. This is just as strong in Bruce as it is in Calvin or in any of the Church Fathers which both loved to cite. In this the concern centres not only in the substitutionary and represent-ative act of Christ on our behalf on the Cross, and in the imputation of Christ's righteousness which not only declares but constitutes us God's justified children, but also in the Humanity of the incarnate Son of God who in His own Person *is* our whole salvation. Holy and eternal life from God resides in the Humanity of Christ, and we are given to share in it as we are united to Christ. Through the Holy Spirit we are made members of Christ and of his Body, and so share in his sanctified human nature and are nourished with the life of God residing in his flesh. In other words, this is the doctrine that the constitution of the Person of Christ, the Mediator, belongs to the essence of his atoning reconciliation, that the atonement involves not only the *act of God* in Christ reconciling the world to himself, but the *human obedience and life* of Jesus the Servant of the Lord and the Son of the Father. It was because Calvin and Bruce grasped the proper place in our salvation of the obedient humanity of the crucified and risen Jesus that they gave

23

it full place in the doctrine of Holy Communion as our sharing through the power of the Spirit in 'the flesh of Jesus', and therefore as our quickening and nourishment with the new humanity God has provided for us in Christ.

It is clear, therefore, that behind the teaching of Bruce in these sermons on the Lord's Supper there lay a powerful and adequate conception of the Person and saving work of Christ, which is perfectly in line with that taught by Calvin. A very interesting passage in this connection is to be found in Bruce's sixth sermon on Isaiah 38, published in 1591, which is very enlightening for our understanding of this conception of union with Christ in the Sacrament. In discussing the salvation that Christ has wrought for us as God and as Man, the only Mediator between God and man, he had this to say:—

'*First*, He delivered us from the sins which we call actual, by the perfect satisfaction whereby He satisfied fully, in suffering hell in His soul, and death in His body, on the Cross, and so freed us from actual sins, and their punishment. In this work He is a perfect Mediator.' This is the aspect of Christ's atoning work which the theologians spoke of as His *passive obedience*. Then, in the third place, Bruce went on to speak of that aspect which the theologians called Christ's *active obedience*.

'Now in the *third place*, also, He is perfect Mediator, for He not only satisfied for our sins, but He fulfilled the whole Law for us, and indeed more than the Law required, for the Second Table requires only that we love our neighbours as ourselves. But Christ did more than this, for no one so loves his neighbour that he will willingly die for him. Christ, in dying for us, showed that He loves us more than the Law requires. Therefore,

24

not only has He fulfilled the Law for us, but done more than the Law demanded. Now this perfect righteousness of His intervenes between us and the Father, and covers our rebellion and disobedience; otherwise, we would not be free from condemnation here either.'

These are the two aspects that cover the atoning work of Christ in scholastic Calvinism, His passive and active obedience on our behalf. But Bruce, following Calvin, could not be content with that, and so between these two he expounded another, and no less essential, main aspect of Christ's atoning reconciliation. And this is what he had to say about it:—

'*Secondly*, He delivered us from the disorder and rotten root from which we proceed. For, as you see, Christ Jesus was conceived in the womb of the Virgin, and that by the mighty power of His Holy Spirit, so that our nature in Him was fully sanctified by that same power. And this perfect purity of our nature in His Person covers our impurity, for He was not conceived in sin and corruption as we are, but by the power of the Holy Spirit, who perfectly sanctified our nature in Him, even in the moment of His conception. Thus in that He was thoroughly purged, His purity covers our impurity.'

If Bruce thought of the satisfaction of Christ as freeing us from our actual sins, it is clear that he thought of His perfect purity in incarnation and birth as covering our original sin, or as sanctifying our human nature. This stress upon incarnational redemption in Christ Bruce sandwiched in between his accounts of Christ's passive and active obedience, for it belongs to the very heart of His saving work. And so he summed it up by saying that all these, namely, perfect satisfaction, perfect purity and perfect righteousness are to be found in Christ perfectly.

It is in this 'whole Christ' that we are given to participate in the Sacrament of the Lord's Supper, and therefore we are given to share not only in the benefits of His death on the Cross and in His righteous fulfilment of the Will of God, but also in His sanctified human nature so that we are sanctified in the purity of His Incarnation through union with Him in His humanity.

This doctrine of saving and sanctifying union with Christ was not peculiar to Bruce in the Church of Scotland. It forms an essential and important element in the *Scots Confession* of 1560; it is clearly and beautifully set forth in the three great Catechisms officially authorised and used by the Kirk before they were unfortunately displaced by the Westminster Divines, namely, Calvin's *Geneva Catechism*, the *Heidelberg Catechism*, and *Craig's Catechism*. It is significant that the last named, indigenously and so characteristically Scottish, written by John Craig, Bruce's Colleague in the Canongate, was enjoined by the Assembly of 1592, over which Bruce presided as Moderator, 'to be made use of in all families and schools.' It is to that Catechism, as well as to the other two, that we must turn if we would have a fuller account of the theology that lies behind Bruce's Sermons. If anything, Bruce's conception of the Lord's Supper in these Sermons is a little more subjective than in any of those Catechisms, which is to be explained not only by the fact that it is expounded by him in preaching, but by the fact that it is influenced by his characteristic preaching direct to the conscience and by his emphasis upon the feeling of the divine Mercy. But in spite of that, in his sermons the doctrine of union with the whole Christ as objective and subjective reality, is expounded as powerfully and clearly as anywhere else in

26

the Fathers or the Reformers. In this work Robert Bruce has left us a legacy which, in the words of the editor of the 1614 edition, is 'worthy to be written in letters of gold'.

To the
Most High, Puissant, and Christian Prince,
JAMES THE SIXTH, KING OF SCOTS,
Grace and Peace from God the Father, and our Lord
Jesus Christ

PLEASE YOUR MAJESTY,—I was not of mind, at the first, that this work should have come out in my time; for the conscience of my own weakness testifies unto me, that nothing worthy of light can proceed from such a one. Yet, notwithstanding, being overcome, at the last, by the instant suit of our Kirk and Session, I was content that their authority should command me in this. And if it shall please the Lord to bless it in such sort, that poor and simple ones may find either comfort or instruction in it, suppose learned ears find no contentment, I will think myself abundantly satisfied. For, seeing God has sanctified me, in some measure, to his work, it must be an argument of his everlasting blessing, that if, while life lasteth, it may be employed always to the profit of his Kirk; for who am I, that should not employ his own graces to his own glory? And I pray God, that it may be found, in that great day, that how mean that ever they be, yet they were accompanied with this special grace, that they were well used. And suppose ye be a King, Sir, of this kingdom presently, and apparent of another, yet think with yourself that all your magnificence, honour, wealth, liberty, and all the rare gifts which God, of his mercy, has planted in you, cannot be otherwise well employed, except they be employed to the defence of the truth, and of that pure and sincere discipline grounded thereupon, which, to your Majesty's great praise, and to our singular comfort, has this long time, by your

Majesty's authority, been established in this country: for this sort of doing shows that God has not only made you an heir to earthly kingdoms, but also has appointed you to be a fellow-heir with Jesus Christ, of that immortal kingdom and glorious Crown that cannot fade or fall away. And as your Majesty's life and liberty has hitherto been conjoined with the standing and liberty of Jesus Christ's kingdom within your country, continue and stick by this liberty, and, no doubt, Jesus Christ shall stick by you. I will not fash your Majesty with many words; only this I do your Majesty, to wit, that I clothe not this work with your Majesty's name and authority for any worthiness that I thought to be in it—for it is rudely set out in sensible and homely terms, as it was received of my mouth, and as it pleased God for the time to give me it; but I had this respect, that as it is the first thing that proceeds from me, so I thought meet to make it the first testimony of my thankfulness and sincere affection, as well to the truth of God as to your Majesty's service, whom, under God, I tender as mine own life, and would be glad that God would bless me with the influence that might advance your Highness' name or estimation, both here in this present world, as in the world to come. And, in the meantime, because I may not as I would, I shall do as I may, in my prayers continually remember your Royal person, together with the Queen your bed-fellow; and crave continually of your race, at the hands of the Almighty God, through the righteous merits of Jesus Christ; under whose protection, for now and ever, I leave your Majesty. From Edinburgh, the 9th of December 1590.

Your Majesty's most humble and obedient subject,

Mr ROBERT BRUCE,
Minister of Christ's Evangel.

THE SACRAMENTS IN GENERAL

For I have received of the Lord that which also I delivered unto you, that the Lord Jesus the night in which He was betrayed, took bread...

I CORINTHIANS 11:23.

THERE is nothing in this world, or out of this world, more to be wished by everyone of you than to be conjoined with Jesus Christ, and once for all made one with Him, the God of glory. This heavenly and celestial conjunction is procured and brought about by two special means. It is brought about by means of the Word and preaching of the Gospel, and it is brought about by means of the Sacraments and their ministration. The Word leads us to Christ by the ear; the Sacraments lead us to Christ by the eye: of the two senses which God has chosen as most fitting for the purpose of instructing us and bringing us to Christ. That doctrine must be most effectual and moving which awakens and stirs up most of the outward senses, for that which awakens not only the ear, but the eye, the taste, the feeling, and all the rest of the outward senses must move the heart most and will pierce into the soul. And so it is. This doctrine of the Sacraments moves, stirs up and awakens most of the outward senses. Therefore, if we come to it well prepared, it must be most effectual in stirring up the inward senses of the dull heart. But there is one thing that you must always remember: there is no doctrine either of the simple Word or of the Sacraments, that is able to move us if Christ takes away His Holy Spirit. Therefore whenever you come to hear the doctrine, whether it be of the Sacraments or of the simple Word, ask that God may be present by His Holy Spirit. Otherwise all the doctrine on earth will not avail you. Nevertheless, this doctrine of the Sacraments stirs up and awakens most of the outward senses, and there is no question, therefore, but that it is an effectual and potent instrument to awaken, prepare and stir up our hearts.

The meaning of the word 'Sacrament'

To show you what the Word 'Sacrament' means, and to remove any ambiguity, let me recall the fact (which is unquestionably true) that the most ancient Latin theologians interpreted the Greek word *mysterion* by the word *sacrament*. They used the Greek word 'mystery' not only to signify the whole action, i.e. the whole action of Baptism and the whole action of the Lord's Supper, but to signify whatever is dark and hidden in itself, and not employed in the common use of men. In this way the Apostle calls the vocation of the Gentiles a 'mystery' (Eph. 3:9). This union which is begun here between us and Christ, is called a 'mystery' (Eph. 5:32), and the Latin interpreters call it a 'sacrament.' In short, you will not find in God's Book a word more frequent than the word 'mystery.' As to the word 'sacrament,' however, by which they translate the Greek word, we do not find it much used by the same theologians, nor is it used so much in any part of God's Book. Nevertheless, the word 'sacrament' is very ambiguous in itself, which has led to disastrous consequences that have not yet come to an end, and will not, as long as the world lasts. If they had kept the Apostle's words, and called the Sacraments 'signs' and 'seals', all this controversy, strife and contention would probably not have occurred; but where men will be wiser than God, and give names to things, relying not on God but on the wisdom of man, which is mere folly, all this trouble comes to pass.

'Sacrament' used in four senses

To come to the point, then, the ancient theologians took the word *Sacrament* apparently in a four-fold way. Sometimes they took it for the whole action, that is for the whole ministry of the elements. Then sometimes they took it not for the whole action, but for the outward things that are used in the action of Baptism, and the Supper, i.e. for the water and its sprinkling, for the bread and wine and their breaking, distributing and eating. Thirdly, they took it not for all the outward things that are used in the action, but only for the material and earthly things, the elements, such as bread and wine in the Supper, and water in Baptism. It is in this sense that Augustine says: 'The wicked eat the Body of our Lord, concerning the Sacrament only, that is, concerning the elements only.' Finally, they took it not only for the elements, but for the things signified by the elements. It is in this sense that Irenaeus says that a Sacrament consists of two things, the one earthly, the other heavenly. In these ways the ancients used the word, and there can be no question that they used it rightly.

Word and Sacrament must always be joined

Leaving the ambiguity of the word, I take the word *Sacrament* as it is taken and used today in the Church of God, for a holy sign and seal that is annexed to the preached Word of God to seal up and confirm the truth contained in the same Word, but in such a way that I do not call the Seal separated from the Word, the Sacrament. There cannot be a Seal except that which is the seal of an evidence, for if the seal is separated from the evidence, it is not a seal, but simply what it is by nature and nothing more. Thus there cannot be a Sacrament without it adhering to the evidence of the Word. Think of what a Sacrament is by nature. It is nothing more than what it actually is by nature. Was it a common piece of bread? It remains common bread, except that it is joined to the evidence of the Word. Therefore the Word alone cannot be a Sacrament nor the element alone, but Word and element must together make a Sacrament. Well has Augustine said: 'Let the Word come to the element and you shall have a Sacrament.' Thus the Word must come to the element, that is, the Word preached distinctly and opened up in all its parts must go before the Sacrament, which hangs on to it; and the Sacrament, as a Seal, must follow and be appended to it. Thus I call a Sacrament the Word and Seal conjointly, the one joined on to the other.

There is no controversy or debate about the fact that all Sacraments are Signs. Now if a Sacrament is a sign, since the sign is in a relation (for we must speak of it in that category), then the Sacrament must be placed in that same category of relation. Now every relation must necessarily involve two things: for one thing cannot be the correlative of itself, but in every proper relation there must be two things with a mutual respect the one for the other. Take away one of these two things from the Sacrament, and you lose the relation, and losing the relation, you lose the Sacrament. Confound one of these two with the other, make either a confusion or mixture of them, and you lose the relation and losing the relation, you lose the Sacrament. Convert the one into the other so that the substance of the one escapes and vanishes in the other, and you lose the relation, and so lose the Sacrament. Therefore as in every Sacrament, there is a relation, in order to keep the relation you must keep the two things distinct in the Sacrament.

Now for the better understanding and consideration of these two diverse things which are relative to one another, we shall by God's grace keep this order. *First*, I shall show you what is meant by a sign in the Sacrament; *next*, I shall explain to you what is meant by the thing signified; *thirdly*, I shall show how these two are coupled together, by what power and virtue they are conjoined, and from whence their power and virtue flow. Fourthly, and finally, I shall explain to you whether one and the same instrument gives the sign and the thing signified, or not; whether they are given in one action or two, whether they are offered to one instrument or two, or if they are given in one or two ways to both instruments. Mark these diversities, the diversity of reception, the diversity of the instruments, and the diversity of the givers, and you will find little difficulty in the Sacrament.

1. The meaning of a sign in the Sacrament

Let us begin with the signs. Since all Sacraments are signs, what do we call the signs in the Sacrament? I call the signs in the Sacrament whatever I perceive and take up by my outward senses, by my eye especially. Now in this Sacrament as you see, there are two sorts of things subject to the outward senses, and especially to the eye. The elements of bread and wine are subject to the eye, therefore they must be signs; moreover, the rites and ceremonies by which these elements are distributed, broken and given, are also subject to the eye. There must therefore be two sorts of signs: one sort, the bread and wine, which we call elemental; another sort, the rites and ceremonies, by which they are distributed, broken and given, which we call ceremonial. Do not be deceived with the word 'ceremony'; do not think that I call the breaking of the bread and drinking of the wine 'ceremonies'. Do not think that they are vain, as when you use the word ceremony for vain things, which has no grace or profit attached to it. No, although I call them ceremonies, every ceremony which Christ instituted in the Supper is as essential as the bread and wine are, and you cannot leave out one jot of them without perverting the whole institution; for whatever Christ commanded to be done, whatever He spoke or did in that whole action, is essential, and must be done. You cannot omit an iota of it without perverting the whole action.

The reason why I call them signs is this: I do not call them signs for the reason that men commonly call them signs, because they only signify something, as the bread signifies the Body of Christ, and the wine signifies the Blood of Christ; I do not call them something because they only represent something. I call them signs because they have the Body and Blood of Christ conjoined with them. Indeed, so truly is the Body of Christ conjoined with the bread, and the Blood of Christ conjoined with the wine, that as soon as you receive the bread in your mouth (if you are a faithful man or woman) you receive the Body of Christ in your soul, and that by faith. And as

35

soon as you receive the wine in your mouth, you receive the Blood of Christ in your soul, and that by faith. It is chiefly because of this function that they are instruments to deliver and exhibit the things that they signify, and not only because of their representation are they called signs. For if they did nothing but represent or signify a thing absent, then any picture or dead image would be a Sacrament, for with every picture, the thing signified comes into your mind. For example, at the sight of a picture of the King, the King will come into your mind, and it will signify to you that that is the King's picture. If, therefore, the sign of the Sacrament did no more than that, all pictures would be Sacraments; but the Sacrament exhibits and delivers the thing that it signifies to the soul and heart, as soon as the sign is delivered to the mouth. It is for this reason, especially, that it is called a sign. No picture of the King will deliver the King to you; there is no other image that will exhibit the reality of which it is the image; therefore no image can be a Sacrament. Thus it is chiefly because the Lord has appointed the Sacraments as hands to deliver and exhibit the things signified, that they are called signs. As the Word of the Gospel is a mighty and potent instrument for our everlasting salvation, so the Sacrament is a potent instrument appointed by God to deliver to us Christ Jesus for our everlasting salvation. For this spiritual meat is dressed and served up to us in spiritual dishes, that is, in the ministry of the Word, and in the ministry of the Sacraments, and though this ministry is external, yet the Lord is said to deliver spiritual and heavenly things by these external signs. Why? Because He has appointed them as instruments whereby He will deliver His own Son to us; for this is certain, that no one has power to deliver Christ Jesus to us, but God Himself, and His Holy Spirit. And therefore, properly speaking, no one can deliver Christ except God Himself by His own Spirit.

He is delivered by the ministry of the Holy Spirit. It is the Holy Spirit who seals Him up in our hearts, and confirms us more and more in Him, as the Apostle says of Him (2 Cor. 1:22).

Strictly speaking, no one has power to deliver Christ but God the Father, or He Himself. No one has power to deliver the Mediator, but His own Spirit. Nevertheless, it has pleased God to use some instruments and means by which He would deliver Christ Jesus to us. The means are these: the ministry of the Word, and the ministry of the Sacraments; and because He uses these as means to deliver Christ, they are said to deliver Him. But here you have to distinguish between the principal efficient deliverer, and the instrumental efficient deliverer, which is the Word and Sacraments. If we keep this distinction, both these are true: God by His Word, and God by His Spirit, delivers Christ Jesus to you. I call them signs, then, because God has made them potent instruments to deliver the same thing that they signify.

2. What is meant by the thing signified

I come now to the thing signified, and I call the thing signified by the signs of the Sacrament, which Irenaeus, that old writer, calls the heavenly and spiritual thing, namely, *the whole Christ with His whole gifts, benefits and graces*, applied and given to my soul. I do not call the thing signified by the signs of bread and wine the benefits of Christ, the graces of Christ, or the virtue that flows out of Christ only, but I call the thing signified together with the benefits and virtues flowing from Him, the very substance of Christ Himself, from which this virtue flows. The substance with the virtues, gifts and graces that flow from the substance, is the thing signified here. As for the virtue and graces that flow from Christ, it is not possible for you to partake of the virtue that flows from His substance, without first partaking of the substance itself. For how is it possible for me to partake of the juice that flows out of any substance without first partaking of the substance itself?

Can my stomach be refreshed with meat, the substance of which never comes into my mouth? Can my thirst be slaked with drink, which never passes down my throat? Can I suck virtue out of anything without first getting the substance? Thus it is impossible for me to get the juice and virtue that flow out of Christ without first getting the substance, that is, Christ Himself.

I do not, therefore, call the thing signified the grace and virtue that flow from Christ only, nor Christ Himself and His substance without His virtue and graces, but the substance together with the graces. It is the whole Christ, God and Man, without separation of His natures, without distinction of His substance from His graces, that I call the thing signified by the signs in the Sacrament. Why is that? If no more is signified by the bread than the Flesh and Body of Christ alone, and no more is signified by the wine than the Blood of Christ alone, you cannot say that the Body of Christ is Christ; for it is but a piece of Christ; nor can you say that the Blood of Christ is the whole Christ, for it is but a part of Him. It was not a piece of your Saviour that saved you, nor was it a part of your Saviour, that wrought the work of your salvation, and so, even should you get a piece of Him in the Sacrament, that would do you no good. Therefore, in order that the Sacrament may nourish you to life everlasting, you must get in it your whole Saviour, the whole Christ, God and Man, with all His graces and benefits, without separation of His substance from His graces, or of the one nature from the other. And how do I get Him? Not by my mouth. It is vain to think that we will get God by our mouth, but we get Him by faith. Since He is a Spirit, I eat Him by faith and belief in my soul, not by the teeth of my mouth—that would be folly. I grant that you might eat the Flesh of Christ with your teeth, and that would be a cruel way of acting, yet you may not eat the Godhead with your teeth. That is a gross way of speaking. So, if ever you are to get good out of the Sacrament, you must get the whole Christ. Moreover, there is no instrument with which you may lay hold of Him, but faith. Therefore come to the Supper with a faithful, i.e. a believing, heart.

The Flesh of Christ is spiritual nourishment

Oh, but you will ask me (and apparently the definition laid down of the thing signified gives grounds for it): If the Flesh of Christ, and the Blood of Christ are a part of the thing signified, how can I call His Flesh a spiritual and heavenly thing? And Christ, in respect of His Flesh, a heavenly thing? You do not say that the substance of Christ's Flesh is spiritual, or that the substance of His Blood is spiritual. Why then do you call it a heavenly and spiritual thing? I will tell you. The Flesh of Christ is called a spiritual thing, and Christ is called spiritual, in respect of His Flesh, not that His Flesh is become a spirit, or that the substance of His Flesh has become spiritual. No, it remains true Flesh and the substance of it is the same as it was in the womb of the Virgin. Nor is His Flesh called spiritual because it is glorified in the heavens at the right hand of the Father. Do not be deceived about that, for even if it is glorified, yet it remains true Flesh, the same Flesh which He took out of the womb of the Virgin. Nor is it spiritual, because you do not see it in the Supper. If you were where it is you might see it; but it is called spiritual because of the spiritual end which it serves for my body and soul, because the Flesh and Blood of Christ serve to nourish me, not for a temporal life, but for a spiritual and heavenly life.

Now, because this flesh is a spiritual food, ministering unto my spiritual life, therefore it is called a spiritual thing. If it nourished me as the flesh of animals does, only for a temporal life, it would be called but a temporal thing. But because it nourishes my soul, not for an earthly and temporal life, but for a heavenly, celestial and spiritual end, the Flesh of Christ, and Christ, in respect of His Flesh, is called the spiritual thing in the Sacrament. It is also called the spiritual thing in the Sacrament because of the spiritual instrument by which it is received. The instrument by which the Flesh of Christ is received is not a corporal instrument, not the teeth and mouth of the body, but spiritual, the mouth of the soul, which is faith. Because the instrument is spiritual, Christ who is received, is also called spiritual. Again, because the mode of reception is a heavenly, spiritual and celestial mode, not a natural or external mode, because the Flesh of Christ which is given in the Sacrament is received in a spiritual and secret way, which is not seen by the eyes of men, therefore for these reasons I call Christ Jesus the heavenly and spiritual thing which is signified by means of the signs in the Sacrament.

The Triune God must apply the thing signified

Now in the end, the thing signified must be applied to us. What help is it to me to see my medicine in a box, standing in an apothecary's shop? What can it do for me, if it is not applied? What help is it to me, to see my salvation far off, if it is not applied to me? Therefore, it is not enough for us to see Christ but He must be given to us, or else He cannot produce health and salvation in us. And since this salvation is given to us, we must have a mouth with which to take it. What help is it to me to see meat in front of me unless I have a mouth with which to take it? So, the thing signified in the Sacrament must be given to us by God, by the three persons of the Trinity, one God. It must be given by Christ Jesus, who must give Himself, and since He gives Himself, we must have a mouth through which to receive Him. Though He presents and offers Himself, yet He cannot profit or help any except those who have a mouth to receive Him. You see then what I call the thing signified: the whole Christ, applied to us and received by us, the whole Christ, God and Man, without separation of His natures, without distinction of His substance from His graces, all applied to us.

We must approach the Lord's Table confessing our need of mercy

Therefore, seeing that we come to the Sacrament to be fed by His Flesh and refreshed by His Blood, to be fed for a heavenly and spiritual life, and seeing that there is no profit to be had at this Table without some kind of preparation, let no man presume to go to the holy Table without in some measure being prepared. Some will be prepared in a greater measure than others; nevertheless, let no man presume to go to it except with a heart in some measure sanctified. Therefore my exhortation concerning the way in which every one of you should prepare yourselves and so enable you better to come to the Table, is this: Not one of you comes to the Table of the Lord to bring before Him your integrity, justice and uprightness. Whoever goes to the Table ought to go acknowledging and confessing his need. He ought to go with a sorrowful heart, for the sins wherein he has offended God; he ought to go with a hated of those sins, not to protest that he is holy, just and upright, but to protest and confess that he is miserable, and of all creatures the most miserable. And therefore he goes to the Table to get strength in his misery, to lay hold upon mercy at the throne of grace, to get remission and forgiveness of his sins, to get the gift of repentance, that more and more he may seek to live uprightly, holily and soberly all his days.

Therefore, unless you have entered upon this course and are determined so to continue with it, to amend your past life, to repent of your sins, and by the grace of God, to live more uprightly and soberly than you have done, for the sake of God, do not go to the Table. Where there is no purpose to do well and to repent, there must of necessity be a purpose to do ill. Whoever comes to this Table with an evil purpose and without intending to repent, he comes to mock Christ, to scorn Him to His face, and to eat his own present condemnation. Thus, let no man come to this Table who does not purpose in his heart to do better, who has not a heart to sorrow for his past sins, and who makes light of his past folly and madness. Let no one come to the Table without such a purpose of repentance, under pain of judgement. But if you have in your heart some purpose to do better, although your former life has been dissolute and loose, and if you are touched in your heart with any feeling or remorse for your past life, do not go away from the Table, but come protesting your misery and wickedness, come with a heart to receive grace. But if you come with a dissolute life (I am not speaking of public wickedness) and do not intend to amend, but continue in sin, then for God's sake abstain.

Much still to be explained

So far we have been dealing with the thing signified. Under this general consideration, there are still several things to explain to you. First, how the signs and the thing signified are coupled together, how they are conjoined. Next, there remains to be told how the sign is delivered, and how the thing signified is delivered, and how both are received, as well as delivered. Then, I shall speak shortly of the other part of the Sacrament, which is the Word, and last of all, I shall show you the mistakes which pervert the Sacrament, and make it of no effect. And if there is time, I shall say something about this Sacrament which we have in hand.

3. The sign and that signified are coupled together

To return, then, it falls to be considered how the signs and the thing signified are coupled together. It is with this conjunction that the whole debate is concerned; all the strife that we have had with those who vary from the strict truth is concerned with the mode of this conjunction. Some insist that the sign and the thing signified conjoin in one way, and some in another way; and people strive very bitterly about this matter, and continue to strive in such a way that through the bitterness of their contention, they lose the truth. For when the heat of contention arises, and especially in

43

debate, they are not concerned for the truth, but for victory. As long as they are victorious, even if it is only through a multitude of words, they do not care even if they lose the truth. Read their works and their books about this conjunction, and you will discover neither conscience nor knowledge. Even if they had a quarter of the conscience that they have of knowledge, this controversy might easily be wound up. But when men lack conscience, and have knowledge, an evil conscience perverts their knowledge, and draws them to an evil end.

The spiritual conjunction of Christ and the believer

To tell you now how these two are conjoined, it will be far easier for me, and better for you to understand, if I tell you first how they are not conjoined: I shall make it very clear to you in that way, but it is not possible to show you so clearly how they actually are conjoined. You may perceive clearly by your own eyes that the sign and the thing signified are not locally conjoined, that is, that they are not both in one place. You may perceive also by your outward senses that the body of Christ, which is the thing signified, and the signs, are not joined corporally; their bodies do not touch one another. You may perceive also that they are not visibly conjoined; they are not both subject to the outward eye. It is easy, then, to let you see how they are not conjoined, for if the sign and the thing signified were visibly and corporally conjoined, what necessity would there be for a sign? To what end would the sign in the Sacrament serve us? Is not the sign in the Sacrament appointed to lead me to Christ, and to point out Christ to me? If I saw Him present with my own eye, as I see the bread, what need would I have of the bread? Therefore you may see

44

clearly that there is no such thing as a corporal, natural, or any such physical conjunction between the sign and the thing signified. And so I say it is easy to let you see how they are not conjoined.

How are they conjoined, then? We cannot ask here, for any other kind of conjunction than that which corresponds and agrees with the nature of the Sacrament. For one thing cannot be conjoined with another thing in any other way than its nature will allow. Therefore, there can be no conjunction here, other than what the nature of the Sacrament will allow. Now the nature of the Sacrament will allow a sacramental conjunction.

Every Sacrament is a mystery. There is no Sacrament but contains a high and divine mystery. Because a Sacrament is a mystery, then, it follows that a mystical, secret and spiritual conjunction corresponds well to the nature of the Sacrament. Since the conjunction between us and Christ is full of mystery, as the Apostle shows us (Eph. 5:32), it is a mystical and spiritual conjunction that is involved. So doubtless the conjunction between the Sacrament and the thing signified in the Sacrament, must be of the same nature, mystical and spiritual. It is not possible to show you by any ocular demonstration how Christ and we are conjoined. Whoever would understand that conjunction must have his mind enlightened with a heavenly sight; as he has an eye in his head to see corporal things, so he must have in his mind and heart a heavenly eye to perceive this secret and mystical conjunction between the Son of God and us in the Sacrament. So I need not insist any longer: unless you have this heavenly illumination you can understand neither your own conjunction with Christ, nor the conjunction between the sign and the thing signified in the Sacrament.

I maintain, then, as the Sacrament is a mystery, so the conjunction which the Sacrament involves must, without doubt, be a mystical, secret and spiritual conjunction. Moreover, I shall show you by a general deduction that in every Sacrament there are two things which have a relation and mutual respect to one another. Thus a relative conjunction would correspond well to the nature of the Sacrament.

'What kind of conjunction is that?' you ask. I answer, the conjunction that corresponds with their nature, a relative and a respective conjunction, i.e. a conjunction in which the sign has a continual respect to the thing signified, and the thing signified to the sign. Then, you ask, 'What kind of conjunction is there between the sign and the thing signified?' I call it a secret and mystical conjunction, that consists in a mutual relation between the sign and the thing signified.

The conjunction of the Word and the thing signified

Apart from the conjunction between Christ and us, there is another conjunction that may make this conjunction between the sign and the thing signified in the Sacrament, more clear. *This is the conjunction between the word that we hear, and the thing signified by the same word.* Note the kind of conjunction this is between the word which you hear, and the thing signified, that comes into your mind. There is a similar conjunction between the sign that you see, and the thing signified in the Sacrament. You may easily perceive that there is a conjunction by the effect, even though you do not know what kind of conjunction it is. Why? As soon as you hear the word spoken by me, immediately the thing which my word signifies, comes into your mind. If I speak of things past, of things to come, or of things near at hand, no sooner do I speak to you of them than the thing signified comes into your mind, doubtless because there is a conjunction between the word and the thing signified. Thus every one of you may easily perceive that there is a conjunction between the word and the thing signified by the word. For example, although Paris is far away from us, yet if I speak of Paris, the word is no sooner spoken than the town will come into your mind. If I speak of the King, even though he is far away from us, the word is no sooner spoken than the thing signified comes into your mind. This coming of the thing signified into the heart and mind shows you clearly that there is a conjunction between the word and the thing signified by the word.

It is not easy to say what kind of conjunction this is, because the thing signified is not present to the eye, as the word is to the ear. If everything signified were as present to your eye as the word is to your ear, it would be easy to see the conjunction; but since the conjunction is mystical, secret and spiritual, it is hard to make you understand it. Recall, however, the conjunction between the simple word and the thing signified by the word. The same kind of conjunction exists between the Sacrament and the thing signified by the Sacrament, for the Sacrament is nothing else but a visible Word. Why do I call it a visible Word? Because it conveys the signification of it by the eye to the mind. Just as in the audible word the signification of it is conveyed by the ear to the mind, so in the same Sacrament, as often as you see it, you will no sooner see the bread with our eye, than the Body of Christ will come into your mind; you will no sooner see the wine, than with the preaching and exposition of the Sacrament the Blood of Christ will come into your mind.

The analogy between the sign and the thing signified

This conjunction between the sign and the thing signified in the Sacrament consists chiefly in two things. *First*, in a relation between the sign and the thing signified, which arises from the likeness and proportion between these two, for if there were no proportion and analogy between the sign and the thing signified by the sign, there could be no Sacrament nor any relation between them. Thus in the first place this conjunction consists in a relation which arises from a certain similitude and likeness which the one has to the other. This likeness may easily be perceived. Think of how the bread is able to nourish your body for this earthly and temporal life; so the flesh of Christ, signified by the bread, is able to nourish both body and soul to life everlasting. Thus you may perceive some kind of proportion between the sign and the thing signified.

The mutual concurrence of the sign and that signified

Secondly, this conjunction consists in a continual and mutual concurring of the one with the other, in such a way that the sign and the thing signified are offered both together, received together at the same time, and in the same action, the one outwardly, the other inwardly; if you have a mouth in your soul, which is faith, to receive it.

Thus in the second place *the conjunction consists in a joint offering and in a joint receiving*; this is what I call a concurrence. If you ask, then, what kind of conjunction is there between the sign and the thing signified, I answer: it is a relative conjunction, a secret

48

and mystical conjunction, which consists in the mutual relation.

There is only one other thing to be observed here, that while you conjoin these two, the sign and the thing signified, you must beware of confounding them. Beware lest you turn the one into the other, but keep each of them in its own integrity, without confusion or mixture of the one with the other. Thus you have the lawful conjunction required in the Sacrament.

The kindness and goodness of God

The main lesson to be learned from this, as far as I can see, is the lesson of the kindness and goodness of the ever-living God who has invented so many wonderful modes of conjunction, all in order that we might be conjoined to Him, and that this great and mystical conjunction between the God of glory and us may be increased. It is in this conjunction alone that our weal, felicity and happiness in this life and in the life to come, consist: that He is so careful to conjoin Himself with His Word and Sacraments that we, in His Word and Sacraments may be conjoined with Him. If we were moved with the care and love of God expressed in these conjunctions, even though it were ever so feebly on our part, assuredly we should not defraud ourselves of the fruit of that happy conjunction, nor bring it into such distaste and disdain as we do today.

By following and preferring our own pleasures to Christ and His counsel, we have made the stomachs of our souls so bad and ill disposed that they do not receive Him at all, or if He is received, He is not able to tarry. And why? Because a bad stomach is not able to keep Him, for immediately we choke Him, either with the lusts of the flesh, or the cares of this world, so that He is compelled to depart. If Christ is not both eaten and digested, He can do us no good, but this digestion cannot exist where there is not a greedy appetite to receive Him. If you are not hungry for Him, He is not ready for you. I am sure that if everybody in this country were examined by this rule, that no one should receive Christ but he who has a stomach hungry for Him, few would be found to receive Him. I am afraid that we have taken such a loathing and disdain for that heavenly food, that there is no such thing as hunger or appetite for it in our souls.

Our sins rob us of our appetite for Christ

What is the cause of this? I will tell you. Although we have renounced the corporal and gross idolatry in which our fathers were drowned and immersed, and which in some parts men still seek to establish, yet as our way of living in this country and the behaviour of every one of us testifies, there is not a man who has renounced that damnable idol that he has in his own soul, or the invisible idolatry that he has in his own heart and mind. Every man still gives his service to the idol which he has from his very conception and birth, and to which he has addicted and enslaved himself. Do not be surprised, therefore, when you have yielded your service, given your affection, and poured out your heart to that pleasure of yours, your idol, your own lust and mischief—do not be surprised, then, if you have no appetite for Christ, or for that heavenly food. When you have poured out your soul on some villainy and wickedness, and have sent it far afield, how can you recover it and bring it home again to employ it where you should, in Christ Jesus?

Our sins rob us of our appetite for Christ

What is the cause of this? I will tell you. Although we
have renounced the corporal and gross idolatry in which
our fathers were drowned and immersed, and which in
some parts men still seek to establish, yet as our way of
living in this country and the behaviour of every one of
us testifies, there is not a man who has renounced that
damnable idol that he has in his own soul, or the
invisible idolatry that he has in his own heart and mind.
Every man still gives his service to the idol which he has
from his very conception and birth, and to which he has
addicted and enslaved himself. Do not be surprised,
therefore, when you have yielded your service, given
your affection, and poured out your heart to that
pleasure of yours, your idol, your own lust and
mischief—do not be surprised, then, if you have no
appetite for Christ, or for that heavenly food. When you
have poured out your soul on some villainy and
wickedness, and have sent it far afield, how can you
recover it and bring it home again to employ it where
you should, in Christ Jesus?

Therefore let every one in his own rank think of his
own domestic idol, that lodges within his own heart, and
strive to rid himself of it, otherwise you cannot see the
face of Christ, to be a partaker of His kingdom.

There is no other lesson in Christianity than this; this
is the first and the last lesson: to shake off your lust and
affections more and more, and so more and more to
renounce yourself that you may embrace Christ. I grant
that there is greater progress in this with some than with
others. Some profit less, some more in this, but unless in
some measure you cast off yourselves, and whatever you
count most precious in your own eyes, in order to come

to Christ, you are not worthy of Him. This is very hard to do. It is very easy to speak of it, to bid a man renounce his own idol, which I call his affection, but it is not done so soon. Assuredly, the stronger must come in to cast out these affections; yes, one stronger than the devil must come in to drive out the devil, who makes his residence in the affections. Otherwise he will remain there for ever. There are not many, therefore, who have renounced themselves. Examine your own heart when you will: if there is anything in the world you love better than Christ, if you are not ready to leave father and mother, to leave wife and children, or whatever is most dear to you in this world for Christ's sake, you are not worthy of Him. If you are not ready to cast off whatever estranges you from Christ, you are not worthy of Him.

Is this a small matter? If there is no part or power of our souls but is opposed to it, and reacts against this heavenly conjunction, is this an easy thing to cast off and renounce ourselves, in order to come to Christ? There is nothing greater than this known to you; it has not entered into every heart to consider this, for this work of a new creation is ten thousand times greater than the work of our first creation.

The wiles of the devil

Therefore, it is most necessary that every man should take heed to himself for the devil is so crafty in regard to this that he is always erecting some idol or other in our souls, and sometimes under the guise of virtue, which is the most dangerous of them all. In every work that we undertake, even the holiest, he is at our right hand, and interests himself in it. He is not content to deceive you under the guise of virtue, but he is so alert that even in your best moments, when you are engaged in your most virtuous acts, he mixes them with sins, and does all he can to make you lose your profit and lose your reward. For when you are best occupied, he seeks to engender in you an opinion of yourselves and so to defraud God of His glory. Or, on the other hand, he makes you so slack and negligent in doing good deeds that if you do them, you do them coldly, and with such lack of discernment that you are primarily concerned with what is of least importance, and you leave the most important things to the last, like Martha. She was occupied and over-busy with those things which are not so necessary as the things with which Mary was occupied, for she should have preferred first the hearing of the Word, to the preparing of Christ's supper.

This is but to give you an insight into the craftiness of the devil, who either gives us a false opinion of ourselves in doing good, or else makes us do that last which should be first, or he makes us altogether so sluggish and so negligent that we do the work of the Lord coldly. Thus in one way or another he is always at work with us, so that we cannot be half watchful enough. We have to do with principalities and powers, with spiritual wickedness which are above us, and within us also, for there is no man who has corruption within him but Satan is in him too. We cannot therefore be watchful enough, always striving to cast out the devil, to renounce ourselves, and to submit to the obedience of Christ.

So much then for our union and conjunction with Christ.

4. How the sign and the thing signified are delivered

Now, seeing that the sign and the thing signified are diverse, it remains to be considered how the sign is delivered and how the thing signified is delivered; and in what way they are received. Here we have to consider the following questions:

First, whether the sign and the thing signified are delivered unto you by the same man or not; *secondly*, whether the sign and the thing signified are delivered unto you in one action or not; *thirdly*, whether both these are given by one instrument or not; *fourthly*, whether the sign and the thing signified are offered and received in the same way or not. After you have considered all these things, you will find in the end, *first*, that the sign and the thing signified are not given by one person; *secondly*, you will find that they are not given in the same sort of act; *thirdly*, you will find that they are not both offered and given by one instrument; and *fourthly*, you will find that they are not both given and received in the same way. Therefore, in view of this diversity, you should note the diversity between the offerers and the givers; the diversity between the actions, the diversity between the instruments, and the diverse ways of receiving. Make diligent note of all these, and you will find little difficulty in understanding the Sacraments.

[1] First, let me make it clear that *the sign and the thing signified by the sign are not both given by one man*. This you see clearly for yourselves. As for the sign, the bread and the wine, it is the Minister who offers it to you; he gives you the Sacrament. As the sign is an earthly and corporal thing, so it is an earthly and corporal man who gives it. The thing signified, however, is of another nature, for it is a heavenly and spiritual thing; therefore, this heavenly thing is not given by an earthly man; this incorruptible thing is not given by a natural and corruptible man. But Christ Jesus has

locked up and reserved the ministry of this heavenly thing to Himself alone. Therefore, there are two givers in this Sacrament: the Minister gives the earthly thing, Christ Jesus, the Mediator, gives the heavenly thing in this Sacrament. For Christ in giving the earthly thing does not use His own ministry immediately, or the ministry of an angel, but only the ministry of an earthly man. And as for the dispensation of His own Body and Blood, He will not give it either to any heavenly creature, far less to an earthly man, but He keeps this ministry to Himself, and He dispenses His own Body and Blood to whom and when He pleases. Why is that? If any man in the world had power to give Christ's Body and Blood, without doubt he would have power to cleanse the heart and conscience (for the Blood of Christ has this power with it) and consequently he would have power to forgive sins.

Now, it is only God who may forgive sins, and therefore it is not possible for the ministry of the heavenly thing to be in the power of any man. We have an example in John the Baptist (Matt. 3:11). Does he not say, 'The ministry that I have is of the element; I am commanded to administer the element of water only; but the ministry of fire, and of the Spirit, Christ has reserved for Himself'? Do not think, therefore, that you will receive the Spirit from the hands of man; you will receive Him from the hands of Christ Himself alone. Without this inward ministry, the outward ministry is not worth a straw. For even if my outward ministry were the ministry of an angel, and even though Christ were present in the flesh, to minister to you these outward things, unless He conjoined with it the inward ministry of His Spirit, it would have no avail. It may well give cause for accusation and judgement against you in the day of that general assembly, but it will never avail for your salvation. Therefore you ought always to pray that the Lord may water your hearts by His Holy Spirit, as He waters your ears by the hearing of the Word.

[2] *There are, then, two offerers, two persons who offer and give the Sacrament, and the thing signified by the Sacrament*; so these two are offered and given in two actions. Christ, who is the heavenly thing, is offered and given to you by an inward, secret and spiritual action, which is not subject to the outward eye. The sign, again, is offered [by the Minister] and given in an outward action in a corporal and visible way.

[3] As there are two kinds of action, so *there are two kinds of instrument*, with which the sign and the thing signified are offered; for the thing signified, that is Christ, is never offered to the mouth of my body; the Blood of Christ, the Flesh of Christ, the whole Christ, or the Spirit of Christ, is not offered either in the Word or in the Sacrament, to the mouth of my body. Show me any passage in the Bible where another way of receiving Christ than by faith is to be found. As I told you, there is no instrument, either hand or mouth, by which we may lay hold of Christ, but faith alone. *As Christ, who is the thing signified, is grasped by the hand and mouth of faith, so the sign, which signifies Christ, is grasped by our own natural mouth and hand.* You have a mouth in your heads, and in your bodies, which is the proper instrument by which to lay hold of the sign; as faith is the proper instrument by which to lay hold of Christ. Thus the sign and the thing signified are offered and given, not to one instrument, but to two, the one to the mouth of the body, the other to the mouth of the soul.

[4] Now see how these things are offered and given: in the same way that they are received. As the sign is corporal and naturally offered to a corporal instrument, so it is received in a corporal and natural way, for you must take the bread and wine either by your hands, or by your mouth. However, the thing signified is not taken in a corporal way, but in a secret and spiritual way. It is taken in the same way in which it is offered. There can be nothing clearer than this: *the one is taken in a natural way, the other in a secret and spiritual way.*

Hence, this is what you must do:—distinguish between the outward and the inward action, between the sign and the thing signified, and keep a proportion and analogy between the inward and the outward actions. You may be quite sure that if you are faithful, Christ is as busy working inwardly in your soul, as the Minister is working outwardly in regard to your body. See how busy the Minister is in breaking the bread, in pouring out the wine, in giving the bread and the wine to you. Christ is just as busy, in breaking His own Body unto you, and in giving you the juice of His own Body in a spiritual and invisible way. Preserve this distinction then and you may assure yourself that by faith Christ is as fully occupied with your soul in nourishing it, as the Minister is outwardly with your body. Keep this, and you have the whole Sacrament.

From what we have said, it follows that the Sacrament consists in a twofold or double manner. It consists of two kinds of materials, that is, an earthly matter, and a heavenly matter: the sign, and the thing signified. And as there is a double matter in the Sacrament, so the Sacrament must be handled in a double way, by an outward action, and an inward action. Preserve this distinction between the sign and the thing signified, and you will not easily slip in the understanding of the Sacrament.

The Word in the Sacrament—both a command and a promise

So far, all we have said concerns the elements, but apart from these general considerations, it remains to say something about the Word, which I call the other part of the Sacrament. I mean and understand by 'the Word' to which the elements are annexed, *that which quickens, which serves as its soul, as it were, and gives life to the whole action.* For by the Word and the appointment of Christ in the Word, the Minister knows what is his part, the hearer knows what is his part, and everyone is prepared for his appropriate action, the Minister to deliver, and the hearer to receive. The institution of Christ is the quickening of the whole action, for all the action derives its warrant from the institution set down in His Word.

There are two things to be considered in Christ's institution: A command, and a promise. The command you will find in His words: 'Take, eat.' The command demands and requires obedience. There is also a promise in the institution, and it is contained in these words: 'This is my Body'. As the command requires obedience, so the promise requires belief. Do not come to the Sacrament, therefore, unless you come both in faith and in obedience. If you do not come with a heart ready to obey Christ, at least more than you have been in the habit of doing, you come to your own judgement. And if you bring a heart void of faith, you come to your own judgement. Thus let everyone who comes to the Sacrament, bring with him a heart determined on doing better, that is, to obey and believe Christ better than in the past. Unless you bring these two in some measure, do not come to the Sacrament, for whatever you do apart from faith, can profit you nothing.

So much, then, briefly, for the Word.

Why is the Sacrament joined to the Word?

Now it will be asked, what need is there for the Sacraments and seals to be annexed to the Word? Why are they annexed, seeing we get no more in the Sacrament, than we get in the Word? And do we get as much in the very simple Word, as we get in the Sacrament? Seeing then we get no new thing in the Sacrament, but the same thing that we get in the simple Word, why is the Sacrament appointed to be joined to the Word? It is certainly true that we get no new thing in the Sacrament; we get no other thing in the Sacrament, than we get in the Word. For what more would you ask than really to receive the Son of God Himself? Your heart can neither desire nor imagine a greater gift than the Son of God, who is King of heaven and earth. Therefore I say, what new thing would you have? If you get Him, you get all things with Him. Your heart cannot imagine any new thing beyond Him. Why then is the Sacrament appointed? Not that you may get any new thing, but that you may get the same thing better than you had it in the Word.

[1] *The Sacrament is appointed that we may get a better hold of Christ than we got in the simple Word,* that we may possess Christ in our hearts and minds more fully and largely than we did before, by the simple Word. That Christ may have more room in which to reside in our narrow hearts than He could have by the hearing of the simple Word, and that we may possess

Him more fully, is a better thing. Even though Christ is the same in Himself, yet the better hold you have of Him, the surer you are of His Promise. The Sacraments are appointed that I may have Him more fully in my soul, that I may have the bounds of it enlarged, and that He may make the better residence in me. This no doubt is the reason why these seals are annexed to the evidence of the simple Word.

[2] *The Sacraments also serve to seal up and confirm the truth that is in the Word.* The office of the seal appended to the evidence is not to confirm any other truth, than that which is in the evidence. Although you believed the evidence before, yet by the seals, you believe it better. But even so, the Sacrament assures you of no other truth than that contained within the Word. Nevertheless, because it is a seal annexed to the Word it persuades you better of its truth, for the more the outward senses are awakened, the more is the inward heart and mind persuaded to believe.

Now the Sacrament awakens all the outward senses, such as the eye, the hand, and all the rest. When the outward senses are moved, without doubt the Holy Spirit concurs, moving the heart all the more. The Sacraments are therefore annexed to the Word, to seal up the truth contained in the Word, and to confirm it more and more in your heart. The Word is appointed to work belief, and the Sacrament is appointed to confirm you in this belief, but unless you feel the truth of this inwardly in your heart, unless you have your heart as ready as your mouth, do not think that it will avail you at all.

All the seals in the world will not work unless the Spirit of God concurs and seals the same truth in your heart, that the Sacrament seals outwardly; unless He makes clear the sight of your mind inwardly, and works a feeling in your heart, both Word and Sacrament will lose the fruit and effect which they should have. All the Scriptures are full of this. The whole divine Scripture is to you but 'the letter that kills' unless the Spirit of God concurs to quicken inwardly. Thus your whole endeavour should be to strive to feel Christ alive in your heart, that finding Him in your hearts, and seeing Him in your minds, both Word and Sacraments may be effectual. If not, your souls remain dead, and you are not translated from that death in which you were conceived. Therefore the whole concern of Christians should be, when they see the Sacraments and hear the Word, to find and feel in their hearts and minds, that which they hear and see. This is what I call finding Christ alive in your own soul; this cannot happen unless you sanctify His lodging, for if all the recesses of your soul remain a dunghill, Christ cannot dwell there. Therefore, unless you strive for continual sanctification, and sever yourselves from everything that severs you from Christ, it is not possible for Him to live or dwell in you.

Our faith strengthened and our weakness helped

This is a great lesson, and it is impossible to carry it out unless, as I have said, a stronger one comes in and possesses us, and makes us renounce ourselves. Thus the seals have only been annexed to the Word for our sakes, for God on His part is under no necessity either to swear or to confirm by seals, the thing that He has spoken. His Word is as good as any oath or seal. But it is necessary for our sakes. So great is the weakness in us, that when He has sworn and set His seal to His own Word, we are as near to belief as if He had never spoken

61

a word. Thus to help our belief, our inherent weakness and inability (for we are so incapable by nature of believing anything but what is of ourselves, and the more we lean on ourselves, the further we are from God), to help this astonishing weakness in which we are ready to distrust God in every Word, He has annexed His Sacrament to His Word, and along with His Sacraments, He swears the things that most concern our salvation—as we hear in regard to the priesthood of Christ, in Psalm 110:4.

God does not only speak, He swears, but that is for the sake of our weakness and infirmity. Nevertheless, if He takes away the ministry of His Spirit, all these means will do us no good.

How can the Sacrament be rendered ineffective?

The last question to be considered is: How is the Sacrament perverted and how are we defrauded of its fruit and effect? Faults of two kinds pervert the Sacraments, and defraud us of their profit and use. These are faults either in regard to the form or in regard to the person. Regarding the form: if the essential form is destroyed, we get nothing, for when the Sacrament is robbed of its essential form, it is no longer a Sacrament. There is an essential form in Baptism, and an essential form in the Supper. If they are taken away, you lose the use of the Sacrament. The essential form of Baptism is: '*I baptise thee in the Name of the Father and of the Son, and of the Holy Spirit.*' Leave out one of these three, or do it in the Name of any one of the three Persons, only, and you lose the essential form of Baptism.

In the Lord's Supper, if you leave out the least ceremony, you lose the essential form and so it is not a

Sacrament. In regard to the essential form, I would say that the Papists preserve it in Baptism, although they have brought in trifles of their own, and mixed them up with Baptism but because they keep the substantial form, it is not necessary that those who were baptised under them should be rebaptised. If indeed the virtue of regeneration flowed from the person, it would be something to be considered; but because Christ Himself gives regeneration to whom and when He pleases, so long as the essential form is preserved, it is not necessary that this Sacrament should be reiterated.

Now what are the faults in the person who perverts the Sacrament? The fault may be either in the person of the giver, or in the person of the receiver. (I do not speak of those faults which are common to all, but of those faults which disqualify the person of the giver from being a distributor of the Sacrament, and take the office away from him.) Thus, when the person of the giver is disqualified, in this way, it is without doubt no Sacrament. Again, the fault may be in the person of the receivers. If their children are not in the Covenant, but are outside of it, they are not given the Sacrament. To be sure, if the parents afterwards enter the Covenant, their children may be received, although they were begotten outside of the Covenant. Similarly, in the Lord's Supper, if a man comes with any burden of sin, without intending to repent of the sins with which he is burdened, he ought not to receive it. Thus if you have no purpose of repentance, you lose the use of the Sacrament. It is only this purpose of repentance that allows me in receiving the Sacrament, to receive also its fruit and effect. Everyone, therefore, who goes to the Sacrament, must examine the purpose he has in his heart. Have you a purpose to shed blood, to continue in harlotry, or to commit any other vile sin that is in your heart? And are you not resolved to repent? In showing yourself to be without repentance, you show yourself to be without faith, and consequently you come to your condemnation, and not to your salvation. Examine, then, the purpose of your heart, for if with a dissolute life you have a dissolute purpose, you come to your condemnation.

I had intended to speak more particularly of this Sacrament but because the time has gone and some of you doubtless are to communicate, I will add only this: Remember that you should not address yourselves to this Table unless you find your hearts in some way prepared. The first step in preparation is contrition, sorrowing for sin, a feeling of your own sins, in which you have offended so gracious a God. If you are able, as that woman was by the tears of a contrite heart to wash the feet of Christ, humbly to kiss them, and to lay hold of them, even though you dare not presume so high as to grasp the whole Christ, you are in a proper state of mind. But if you are wanting in all these, if you do not have them in any measure, you are altogether unprepared. Therefore let no one come to this Table unless he has these at least in some measure.

But where there is displeasure for sin, an intention to do better, an earnest sorrow and a yearning to receive the thing which you desire, then in that soul where God has placed this desire for Christ, God's Spirit is at work, and Christ will enter in. Therefore, even if that soul is far from what he should be, let him not refuse to go to the Lord's Table, but let him go professing his own infirmity and weakness, and with the desire for the thing that he seeks. Let every one of you who finds himself disposed in this way, go in God's Name to the Lord's Table. May the Lord work this in every one of your hearts, that this ministry may be effectual in you at this time, through the righteous merit of Jesus Christ, to whom with the Father and the Holy Spirit be all honour, praise and glory, both now and for ever. Amen.

2

THE LORD'S SUPPER IN PARTICULAR 1

For I have received of the Lord that which also I delivered unto you, that the Lord Jesus, the night in which he was betrayed, took bread.

I CORINTHIANS 11:23.

IN our last lesson, Beloved in Christ Jesus, we ended our consideration of the Sacraments in general; now we must turn to the consideration of this Sacrament of the Lord's Supper in particular. In order that you may get to know better and consider the great riches contained in this Sacrament of the Supper, I shall try, as God gives me grace, to put before you certain things to make its understanding easier. *First of all*, I shall show you the names given to the Sacrament in the Bible, and some names given to the Sacrament by the Fathers. *Next*, I shall explain the chief end and reasons why the Sacrament was instituted and appointed by Christ Jesus. *Thirdly*, I shall come to the things contained in the Sacrament: how these are joined together, how they are delivered, and how they are received. And *last of all*, I shall answer certain objections which may be laid against this doctrine, and, as God gives me grace, I shall refute them, and so end this present exercise.

1. Various names given to the Sacrament

In Scripture

Now, we find various names given to the Sacrament of the Supper in God's Book, and every name carries a special reason with it. We find this Sacrament called 'the Body and Blood of Christ'. This name is given to it without doubt because it is a heavenly and Spiritual nutriment; it contains a food for the soul that is able to nourish and build up the soul for a spiritual life for the life everlasting. Thus it is called 'the Body and Blood of Christ'. It is also called 'The Supper of the Lord' to distinguish it from a common supper. This is the Lord's Supper, a holy Supper, not a profane or common supper, but a Supper appointed for the increase of holiness, for the food of the soul in holiness, to feed the soul for the life everlasting. It is not a supper appointed for the physical body, for the Lord had ended the supper for the physical body before He began this Supper which was appointed for the soul, which is called 'Supper' doubtless because it was instituted at the time when they used to sup. It is also called in the Bible 'the Table of the Lord'. It is not called the 'Altar' of the Lord for the Apostle calls it a Table to sit at, not an Altar to stand at, i.e. a Table at which to take and receive, not an Altar at which to offer and present. It is also called 'the Communion and Participation of the Body and Blood of Christ'. These are the names given to it, along with some others in the divine Scriptures.

In the Fathers

The Fathers of the Latin and the Greek Churches gave it various names for various reasons. They called it 'a Public Action', and this was a very general name.

Sometimes they called it 'a Thanksgiving', sometimes 'a Banquet of Love'; sometimes they gave it one name, and sometimes another; and at last, in the declining state of the Latin Church, and in the falling estate of the Roman Church, this Sacrament began to be perverted. With this decay there came in a perverse name, and they called it 'the Mass'. They give themselves a good deal of trouble over the derivation of this name; sometimes they derive it from a Hebrew source, sometimes from a Greek, and sometimes from a Latin source. Judging from the sound of the word, it is clearly to be derived from the Latin. It is a word which might have been tolerable when it was first instituted, for no doubt the Sacrament at the first institution of this word was not wholly perverted. But now, in process of time, corruption has gone so far that it has turned the Sacrament into a sacrifice. Where we should take from the hand of God in Christ, they make us give.

This is plain idolatry; therefore, although the word was tolerable before, it ought not to be tolerated any more. I have no doubt that if we had eaten and drunk the Body and Blood of Christ in our souls as often as we have eaten the bread and drunk the wine, that are signs of His Body and Blood, we should never have allowed this word of the Mass, much less the performance of it, to be so common in this country. But because we have only played the hypocrite, and defrauded our souls of the Body and Blood of Christ, and taken only the outward Sacrament, our zeal decays, and so our knowledge and light decay as well. In default of true zeal, love and knowledge, you have become accustomed to what comes from abusing the word 'Mass', and not only to the word, but to its actual performance. I shall not pursue that further, but only want to tell you what comes from the hearing of the word, and what judgements follow upon this abuse in the reception of the Sacraments.

2. The purpose of the Sacrament

I come next to the ends for which the Sacrament was appointed. The *first* end why Sacrament was instituted in the signs of bread and wine and was appointed chiefly to represent our spiritual nutriment the full and perfect nutriment of our souls. As he who has bread and wine lacks nothing for the full nourishment of his body, so he who partakes of the Body and Blood of Christ, lacks nothing for the full and perfect nourishment of the soul. To represent this full and perfect nourishment, the signs of bread and wine in the Sacrament were ordained and instituted.

The *second* end for which this Sacrament was instituted was this: that we might bear witness to the world and to Princes of the world who are enemies of our profession, that we might openly avow and testify to them our religion and manner of worship, in which we avow and worship Christ, and that we might also testify our love towards His members, our brothers.

The *third* end for which it was instituted is this: to serve as our special comfort and consolation, to serve as a sovereign medicine for all our spiritual diseases, when we find ourselves either ready to fall, or provoked to fall, by the devil, the flesh, or the world; or, after we are fallen and are put to flight by the devil, vainly seek to fly away from God. God in His mercy and in His infinite and bottomless compassion, has set up this Sacrament as a sign upon a high hill, so that it may be seen on every side, far and near, to recall all those who have shamefully run away; and He clucks to them as a hen to a chicken to gather them under the wings of His infinite mercy.

The *fourth* end for which the Sacrament was instituted was this: that in this action we might render to God hearty thanks for His benefits, and since He has come down so familiarly to us, bowed the heavens, as it were, and given us the Body and Blood of His own Son, that we might render unto Him hearty thanks and so sanctify His benefits to us. For this thanksgiving this Sacrament was also instituted.

So much then, briefly, for the ends for which the Sacrament was instituted.

3. The things contained in the Sacrament

Now I come to the things contained in the Sacrament. You see with your eyes that there are corporal things, visible things, such as the bread and wine. There are also hidden from the eye of your body, but present to the eye of your mind, spiritual things, heavenly and inward things. Both these are in the Sacrament.

The corporal, visible and outward things are the things which are appointed to signify the spiritual, heavenly and inward things. Why is that? Everything has a reason. These corporal signs are appointed to signify the spiritual things because they are corporal; we are earthly in body; we have our soul lodging within a carnal body, a tabernacle of clay, a crude tabernacle which cannot be awakened or moved except by things like itself. It cannot be brought to the consideration of heavenly things, except by crude, temporal and corporal things. If we had been of the nature of the thing signified, that is, if as the thing signified is spiritual and heavenly, we had been always spiritual and heavenly, we would not have needed a corporal thing. Again, if the thing signified had been as we are, corporal, earthly and visible, we would not have needed a sign to lead us to consider it. But because the thing signified is spiritual, and we are corporal, therefore in order to bring us to the sight of these spiritual things, God uses corporal means, and an outward sign. This is the reason why these corporal signs are appointed to signify the spiritual things.

The spiritual thing in both the Sacraments is one and the same, Christ Jesus, signified in both the Sacraments, but in different ways. He is the thing signified in Baptism, and He is the thing signified in the Supper. *This Christ Jesus in His Blood chiefly is the thing signified in the Sacrament of Baptism.* Why? Because by His Blood He washes away the filth of our souls; because by virtue of His Blood He quickens us in our souls with a heavenly light, and because by the power of His Blood, He ingrafts and inserts us into His own Body. For that Sacrament is a testimony of the remission of sins, that is of the cleanness of our consciences, of the fact that our consciences are washed inwardly by His Blood. It testifies also to our new birth, that we are begotten spiritually into a heavenly life. It testifies further to our union with the Body of Christ. It is also a seal as well as a testimony. It not only testifies, but seals this up in our hearts, and makes us in our hearts taste the heavenly life already begun in us, i.e. that fact that we are translated from the death in which we were conceived and inserted into the Body of Christ. Note then that Christ in His Blood is the layer of our regeneration, and is therefore the thing signified in Baptism.

In the Sacrament of the Supper, on the other hand, the same Christ is the thing signified in another respect, in that His Body and Blood serve to nourish the soul to life everlasting, this Sacrament is nothing else than the image of our spiritual nutriment, for God testifies in it by the figure of corporal nourishment, how our souls are fed and nourished for the heavenly life. Thus in different ways the same reality, Christ Jesus, is signified in Baptism and in the Supper. In this Sacrament we have the fruits of Christ's death, of which I spoke; the virtue of His sacrifice, the virtue of His passion. I do not call these fruits and virtues alone the thing signified in the Sacrament of the Supper; the thing signified I call rather the substance, and the person out of whose substance this virtue and these fruits flow and proceed.

I grant, and it is certainly true, that by the right use and participation of the Sacrament you partake of all these fruits, nevertheless the fruits themselves are not the first and the chief thing that you partake of in the Sacrament. You must first of all get something else. It is true that no man can partake of the substance of Christ without at the same time partaking also of the fruits that flow from His substance. Nevertheless, you must discern between the substance, and the fruits that flow from the substance, and you must be a partaker of the substance in the first place. Then in the next place you must be a partaker of the fruits that flow from His substance. Let me make this clear. In Baptism, the fruits of the Sacrament are remission of sins, mortification, the slaughter of sin, and the sealing of our adoption to life everlasting.

The substance from which these fruits grow is the Blood of Christ. You must of necessity, therefore, distinguish between the Blood, which is *the substance,* and the remission of sins, the washing and regeneration, which are *the fruits* that flow from His Blood. Likewise, in the Sacrament of the Supper, the fruits of the Sacrament are the growth of faith, and increase in holiness. The thing signified is the substance, that is, the Body and Blood of Christ is the substance, out of which this growth in faith and holiness proceeds.

Now, do you not see that you must discern between the substance and the fruits, and must place the substance in the first place so that the substance of Christ, that is Christ Himself, is the thing signified in the Sacrament? Your own experience makes this clear to you. Before your stomach is filled with any food, you must first eat the substance of the food. Before you are filled with bread, you must first eat the substance of the bread. Before your thirst is quenched with any drink, you must of necessity first drink the substance of the drink. Thus, in the same way before the hunger of your soul is satisfied, and its thirst is quenched, you must first eat the flesh of Christ, and drink His Blood, and that by faith. Try then to understand the one through the other. Consider the use of bread and wine for the body. The Body and Blood of Christ have the same use for your soul. The same God who appointed the one to serve your body, appointed the other to serve your soul. Think of how impossible it is to be fed with food that never comes into your mouth, or to regain your health by medicine that is never applied or procured out of the apothecary's shop. It is just as impossible for you to be fed by the Body of Christ, or to get your health from the Blood of Christ, unless first of all you eat His Body and drink His Blood. Thus you see the thing signified in the Lord's Supper is not so much the fruits of the Sacrament, as the Body and Blood of Christ Jesus, which is the fountain and substance from which all these fruits flow and proceed.

Now, even if Christ, who is the thing signified, remains one and the same in both Sacraments, the signs by which this one Christ is signified in the Sacraments are not the same, nor are they equal in number. In Baptism, the thing that represents Christ is water; in the Supper, the things that represent Christ are bread and wine. Water is appointed to represent Christ in Baptism, because it is most appropriate to represent our washing with the Blood of Christ. What is better to wash with than water? So there is nothing more suitable in which to wash the soul than the Blood of Christ. In the Sacrament of the Lord's Supper, He has appointed bread and wine, because there is nothing more appropriate to nourish the body than bread and wine. Thus the Lord has not chosen these signs without a reason. As the signs in the Sacrament are not always the same, so the signs in the two Sacraments are not the same number. In Baptism, we have but one element; in this Sacrament, we have two elements.

Now what is the reason for this difference, that the Lord has appointed two signs in one Sacrament, and only one sign in the other? I will give you the reason. He has appointed only one sign in Baptism, namely water, because water is sufficient enough for the whole act. If water had not been sufficient to represent the thing signified, He would have appointed another sign, but because water is adequate, and represents fully the washing of our souls by the Blood of Christ, what need do we have for any other sign? Now in this Sacrament of the Lord's Supper, one sign is not sufficient—two are required. Wine cannot be sufficient alone, neither can bread be sufficient alone; for he who only has bread or only wine, does not have a perfect corporal food; therefore, in order that they may represent and show forth a perfect food, God has given us both bread and wine (for the perfect corporal food consists in meat and drink) to represent the full and perfect food of the soul. See how full and perfect nourishment He has for his body who has a store of bread and wine; so he who has Christ has no lack of full and perfect food for his soul. Thus you see the reason why two signs are appointed in this Sacrament, and only one in Baptism.

There remain two further questions concerning these signs, First, what power has the bread in the Sacrament to be a sign, more than the bread used in common houses? Where does that power come from? Secondly, if it has a power, how long does that power endure and remain with the bread?

The power given to the bread by Christ

First let me speak of the power which this bread has beyond that of any other bread. This bread has a power given to it by Christ and His institution, by which it is appointed to *signify* His Body, to *represent* His Body and to *deliver* His Body. This bread has a power deriving from Christ and His institution, which other common bread does not have. Thus, if any of you would ask when the Minister in this action breaks or distributes the bread, pours out and distributes the wine: 'What kind of things are these?' The answer is: they are holy things. This is the name you must give to the signs and seals of the Body and Blood of Christ. *The bread of the Sacrament is a holy bread, and the wine is a holy wine.*

Why? Because the blessed institution of Christ has separated them from the use to which they were put before, and has applied them to a holy use—not to feed the body, but to feed the soul. So much then for the power of this bread: it has a power deriving from Christ and His institution.

For how long does the bread retain this power?

The *second* question is this: How long does this power continue with the bread? How long does the bread have this office? In a word, *this power remains with the bread during the time of the action, during the service of the Table.* See how long that action continues, and the service of the Table lasts: so long does it continue to be holy bread, and so long does the power continue with the bread. But see how quickly the action is ended; the holiness of it ends at the same time. See how quickly the service of the Table is ended; its holiness ceases at the same time, and then the bread becomes common bread again. This power, then, does not continue for ever, but it continues only during the time of the action, and the service of the Table. So much for the elements.

The significance of the bread and wine

Apart from the elements, there is another kind of sign in the Sacrament. Every rite or ceremony in the Sacrament is a sign, and has its own spiritual signification, such as looking at the breaking of the bread, which represents to you the breaking of the Body and Blood of Christ. It is not that His Body was broken in bone or limb, but that it was broken in pain, in anguish and distress of heart, under the weight of the indignation and wrath of God, which He sustained in bearing our sins. Thus the breaking is an essential ceremony, the pouring out of the wine is also an essential ceremony; for, as you see clearly, by the wine is signified the Blood of Christ, so by the pouring out of the wine is signified that His Blood was severed from His flesh. The severing of these two makes death, for in blood is the life. Consequently, it testifies to His death. The pouring out of the wine, therefore, tells you that He died for you, that His Blood was shed for you, so that this is an essential ceremony which must not be omitted. Likewise the distribution, the giving and eating of the bread, are essential ceremonies. And what does the eating testify to you? The application of the Body and Blood of Christ to your soul. Thus every one of these rites has its own signification, not one of them can be left out without perverting the whole action. So much for the signs.

Now what do you learn from all this? Learn this lesson, and you will benefit from these things; because every sign and ceremony has is own spiritual signification, and there is no ceremony in this whole action lacking its own spiritual signification. When you are at the Lord's Table, watching what the Minister does outwardly, in breaking and distributing the bread, in pouring out and distributing the wine, think of this: Christ is as busy doing all these things spiritually to your soul. He is as busy giving to you His own Body, with His own hand; He is as busy giving to you His own Blood, with its power and efficacy. Likewise, in this action, if you are a faithful Communicant, think of what the mouth does, and how the mouth of the body is occupied outwardly; in the same way, the hand and mouth of the soul, which is faith, are occupied inwardly. As your mouth takes the bread and the wine, so the mouth of your soul takes the Body and Blood of Christ, and that by faith. By faith and a constant persuasion is the only way to eat the Body and drink the Blood of Christ inwardly. As you do this, there cannot but follow a fruitful manducation [eating]. So much for our consideration of the signs.

Conjunction of the elements to Christ's Body and Blood

Now we come to the point of greatest difficulty, of which, by the grace of God, I spoke generally in the last sermon, but of which I must now speak more particularly, but more briefly. In order to inform your consciences, and to prepare your souls, you have to understand *how the bread and the wine as signs are joined to the Body and Blood of Christ, as that which they signify.* We must try to understand what kind of conjunction this is, and where it comes from. If you want to know how the two things are conjoined in this way, you must first of all observe the nature of the sign, and the nature of the thing signified. Both their natures must be considered. Why? Because nothing can be coupled or conjoined with any other thing except so far as its nature will allow. If its nature does not allow any conjunction, they cannot be conjoined. On the other hand, if its nature does allow a conjunction, you have to consider how far such a conjunction can be carried through.

First of all then, consider the thing signified, and its nature. Observe that the thing signified is of a spiritual nature, of a heavenly and mystical nature; then conclude without doubt that this spiritual thing will allow a spiritual conjunction, a mystical and secret conjunction. On the other hand, observe the sign, and its nature. The sign by its nature has a relation to the thing signified, and the thing signified by its nature has a relation to the sign. Thus the sign and the thing signified may be conjoined in a mutual relation. Because they have a mutual relation, one to the other, the sign and the thing signified will allow themselves to be conjoined by a relative conjunction.

Now if you ask me what kind of conjunction there is between the bread and the wine, and the Body and Blood of Christ, I will say, it is a secret and spiritual conjunction, with a mutual relation between the bread and the Body of Christ, and between the wine and the Blood of Christ. You would not be so inquisitive of this conjunction if it were corporal, visible or local; if you saw them both before your eyes, you would not ask how they were conjoined, nor if you saw them both in one place. But because you see only the one with your eyes, and the other is hidden, the conjunction is much more difficult to express and understand. How can you understand, comprehend this secret and hidden conjunction, unless the eyes of your mind are enlightened by the Spirit, whereby you may reach a true understanding of it? But if you have any insight into these spiritual matters, which comes by faith, this conjunction will appear as clearly to the eye of your faith as the physical conjunction appears to the eye of your body.

An illustration of conjunction

There is another conjunction which helps to make this conjunction very clear, namely the conjunction between the word which I speak, and the thing signified by the same word. If I speak to you in a language you do not understand, as by God's grace you understand the language I now speak, if I speak of things past, even a short time ago, of things to come, although they are not far off, or of things absent, although they are not so far distant, yet as soon as I speak the word, the thing itself comes into your mind. The word is heard no sooner by your ear, than the thing signified by the same word comes into your mind. What makes the thing signified, even if absent, come into your mind? This would be impossible unless there were a conjunction between the word and the thing signified by the word. For example, if I speak of the King, who is now far away from us (God save him), you will no sooner hear the word, than the King, who is signified by this word, will come into your mind. If I speak of things past, even though they are already expired, yet the thing signified will always come into your mind. Thus there is a conjunction between the word and the thing signified by the word.

From that conjunction you will understand the nature of the conjunction and union between the sign and the thing signified in the Sacrament. Between the Sacrament which is seen by the eye of your body, and the thing signified by the Sacrament, which is seen only by the eye of your soul, there is the same kind of conjunction as there is between the word and the thing signified by the word. For example, as soon as you see the bread taken into the hand of the Minister, immediately the Body of Christ must come into your mind. These two are so conjoined that they come both together, the one to the outward senses, the other to the inward senses. Even this is not enough, for in the institution you are commanded to go further, not only to look at the bread and the wine, but to take the bread and the wine; as soon as your hands take the one, your heart takes the other. As soon as your mouth eats the one, the mouth of your soul, which is faith, eats the other, that is, applies Christ to your soul.

Here then, as you see, there is a secret and mystical conjunction, and therefore Christ cannot be united to you except by a secret and mystical conjunction. This conjunction between Christ and us is the spiritual conjunction which the Apostle spoke of as full of a great mystery (Eph. 5:32). This conjunction cannot be comprehended right away, for since the conjunction is secret and spiritual, and is not to be perceived except through the Spirit of God, all is in vain unless you have some portion and measure of His Spirit. Nothing that is taught in the Word and Sacraments will ever do you good or lift up your soul to heaven, unless the Spirit of God enlightens your mind, and makes you find in your soul the thing that you hear in the Word.

Learn this then, since the Word cannot be understood except by the Spirit of God, ask that the Lord may enlighten the eyes of your mind by His Spirit, and do you on your part be as careful to receive His Spirit as you are now in the hearing of the Word. So far for the conjunction.

Receiving the sign and the thing signified

Now you have heard how the sign is conjoined to the thing signified, it remains for you to know how the sign is received and how the thing signified is received, whether they are both received with the one mouth or not, whether the sign and the thing signified are received in the same way or not. If you note the different ways of receiving and the difference in the instruments, you will not easily err in the Sacrament. The sign and the thing signified are received by two mouths, for you see the signs, that is, the bread and the wine, and to what they are given, namely to the mouth of the body. The mouth of the body is the instrument that receives the bread and the wine, which are the signs. Since the bread and the wine are visible and corporal, the mouth and the instrument by which they are received is visible and corporal. The thing signified by the bread and the wine is not received by the mouth of the body. No, the Scriptures clearly deny that. It is received by the mouth of the soul. There are then two mouths: the bread and the wine, that are the signs, are received by the mouth of the body; Christ, who is the thing signified, is received by the mouth of the soul, that is, by true faith. So, do not bring to the Lord's Table only one mouth (for if you bring the mouth of your body only, all is wrong), but bring with you also the mouth of the soul, that is, a constant persuasion in the death of Christ, and all goes well.

Now, as to the way in which the signs are received, and to the mode in which the thing signified is received, you know well that these corporal and natural signs must be received in a corporal and natural way, they must be taken with the hand, or the mouth of the body; but a supernatural thing, on the other hand, must be received in a supernatural way, a spiritual thing must be received in a spiritual way. Thus as the signs are corporal, and are received in a corporal way, with the hand or the mouth of the body, so the thing signified is spiritual and is received in a spiritual way, with the hand and mouth of the soul, which is true faith. Thus you have briefly given to you all that is required to prepare you for the understanding of the Sacrament.

Now we come to another point. When I say that Christ is the thing signified, and cannot be perceived except by faith, cannot be received or digested except by a faithful soul, what kind of perception do I mean? I do not teach any but a spiritual perception of Christ; He can only be received or perceived by faith, and faith is spiritual. In the Sacrament there is only a spiritual perception, not an oral, carnal or fleshly perception of Christ. That is the fundamental thing; now let us see whether it can be maintained consistently.

The first objection answered

The Papists say that it is not consistent on this ground: *if there is no perception of Christ, except a spiritual perception, then, they say, your Sacrament is in vain. The Sacrament of the Supper was instituted to no purpose.* What is their reason? If there is no way, the Papists say, to perceive Christ except by faith, what need have you of a Sacrament? You perceive Christ by faith in the Word; by the naked and simple preaching of the Word, you get faith. Thus, the simple Word may accomplish it. What need have you of the Sacrament if you do not get something new in the Sacrament which you could not get in the Word? This is their argument, and its conclusion is evident: we get no new thing in the Sacrament other than we get in the Word, if there is no perception but a spiritual one. Therefore, the Sacrament is superfluous.

We admit the antecedent to be true: we do not get any other thing or any new thing in the Sacrament, but we get the same thing which we got in the Word. Try to imagine to yourself what new thing you would have. No matter how much the heart of man conceives, imagines and wishes, he will never dare to think of such a thing as the Son of God. He could never presume to pierce the clouds, to ascend so high, to ask for the Son of God in His flesh to be the food of his soul. If you have the Son of God, you have Him who is the heir of all things, who is King of heaven and earth, and in Him you have all things. What more, then, can you want? What better thing can you wish for? He is equal with the Father, one in substance with the Father, true God and true Man.

What more can you wish? Therefore I say, we get no other thing in the Sacrament than we get in the Word. Content yourself with this. But if this is so, the Sacrament is not superfluous.

Would you understand, then, what new thing you get, what other things you get? I will tell you. Even if you get the same thing which you get in the Word, yet you get that same thing better. What is this 'better'? You get a better grip of the same thing in the Sacrament than you got by the hearing of the Word. That same thing which you possess by the hearing of the Word, you now possess more fully. God has more room in your soul, through your receiving of the Sacrament, than He could otherwise have by your hearing of the Word only.

'What then', you ask, 'is the new thing we get?' We get Christ better than we did before. We get more fully the thing which we had, that is, with a surer apprehension than we had before. We get a better grip of Christ now, for by the Sacrament my faith is nourished, the bounds of my soul are enlarged, and so where I had but a little grip of Christ before, as it were, between my finger and my thumb, now I get Him in my whole hand, and indeed the more my faith grows, the better grip I get of Christ Jesus. Thus the Sacrament is very necessary, if only for the reason that we get Christ better, and get a firmer grasp of Him by the Sacrament, than we could have before.

If it were true that the Sacrament is superfluous, by the same reason it would follow that the repetition of the Sacrament is superfluous, for when you come to the Sacrament the second time, you get no other thing than you did the first time; when you come to the Sacrament the third time, you get no other thing than you did the first time. And yet no one will say that the second and the third comings were superfluous. Why? Because in the second coming my faith is augmented, I understand better, I grow in knowledge, I grow in apprehension, I grow in feeling. Since I grow in all these ways, as often as I come to the Sacrament, no one will say that frequent coming to the Sacrament is superfluous, even if it were once a day. Thus their first charge of inconsistency fails that we get no new thing in the Sacrament, and therefore the Sacrament is superfluous.

The second objection answered

Here there arises another point. If Christ is not perceived, except by faith, then, we say, no wicked person can perceive Him. He who lacks faith cannot perceive Him. He who lacks faith may receive the Sacrament of the bread and wine, and may eat of the bread and wine, but He who lacks faith may not eat of the Body and Blood of Christ, signified by the bread and wine. So this is the ground: no faithless person can receive Christ or eat the Body of Christ in the Sacrament. Against this ground they discharge their artillery, and bring up their argument out of the very words of the Apostle which I have read, namely, 'Whosoever eats this bread, and drinks the cup of the Lord, unworthily, shall be guilty of the body of blood of the Lord.' Their argument, then, takes this form: no man can be guilty of that thing which he has not received. He has not received the Body and Blood of Christ, therefore he cannot be guilty of the Body and Blood of Christ. According to the Apostle, however, he is guilty, therefore he has received the Body and Blood of Christ.

In reply to this proposition, I say: it is very false to say that they could not be guilty of the Body and Blood unless they had received it, for they may be guilty of the same Body and of the same Blood even though they never received it. But look at the text. The text does not say that they eat the Body of Christ unworthily, but it says that they eat the bread and drink the wine unworthily, and yet because they eat the bread and drink the wine unworthily, they are counted before God guilty of the Body and Blood of Christ. Now why is this? Not because they received Him, for if they received Him they could not but receive Him worthily; for Christ cannot be received by anyone except worthily. But they are counted guilty of the Body and Blood of the Son of God, because they refused Him; for when they did eat the bread and drink the wine, if they had had faith, they might have eaten and drunk the Flesh and Blood of Christ Jesus. Now, because they refused the Body of Christ offered to them, they contemn this Body offered to them, if they do not have an eye to discern and judge the Body that is offered to them. If they had had faith, they might have seen His Body offered with the bread; by faith they might have taken that same Body and by faith have eaten it. Therefore, because they lacked their wedding garment, wherein to eat the Body and drink the Blood of Christ, that is, because they lacked faith, which is the eye of the soul to perceive, and the mouth of the soul to receive, the Body which is spiritually offered, they are counted guilty of the Body and Blood of Christ.

Now let me make this clear by an illustration. It is the custom among worldly princes not to allow their majesty to be interested in the smallest thing that they have. What is there that concerns the majesty of a prince of smaller account than a seal, for its substance is only wax? And yet if you use that seal scornfully, if you despise it and stamp it under your feet, you are counted guilty of his body and blood, just as if you had put your hand upon him, and you would be punished accordingly. Much more, if you come as a dumb animal to handle the seals of the Body and Blood of Christ, will you be counted guilty of His Body and of His Blood.

Thus as to the eating of the Body and Blood of Christ, we must say: the wicked cannot eat the body of Christ, but they may be guilty of it. The Apostle makes this clearer still in another passage: in Hebrews 6:6 it is said that the apostates, those who grievously fall away, 'crucify again to themselves the Son of God'. Their falling away makes them as guilty as those who crucify Him. He is now in the heavens, they cannot bring Him down from heaven to crucify Him, and yet the Apostle says that they crucify Him again. Why? Because their malice is as great as theirs who crucified Him, so that if they had Him on earth, they would do the same, therefore they are said to crucify the Son of God. Similarly, in Hebrews 10:29 there is another passage in which the wicked are said to tread the Blood of Christ under their feet. Why? Because their malice is as great as theirs who trod upon His Blood; for this reason they are counted guilty of the Body and Blood of Christ, not because they eat His Body, but because they refuse it when they might have had it.

The time is yet to come when we may receive the Body and Blood of Christ. This is a very precious time. Let us remember that the dispensation of these times is very secret, and has its own limits; if you do not seize this time it will vanish. This time of grace and of the heavenly food has long been dispensed to you; how you have profited from it, your life and behaviour testify. Take hold of yourself in time, redeem the time, for you do not know how long it will last. Ask for a mouth to receive the food of your soul that is offered to you, as well as the food of your body. Seize the time while you have it, or assuredly the time will come when you will cry for it, and will not get it, but instead of grace and mercy, there will come judgement, vengeance, and the dispensation of wrath.

The third objection answered

They will not leave the matter like this. They still insist and bring more arguments to prove that the wicked are partakers of the Body and Blood of Christ. 'You grant,' they say, 'that the bread which the wicked man eats is not naked bread, but the bread of the Sacrament.' Then they argue thus: the Sacrament has always conjoined with it the thing signified; but the Sacrament is given to all, therefore the thing signified is given to all.

What if I grant them this argument? Nothing inconsistent would follow, for the thing signified may be given to all, that is offered to all, as it is offered to all men, and yet not be received by all. *It does not follow that what is given to all is received by all.* I may offer you two things, but it is in your own power whether you will take them or not, but you may take the one, and refuse the other; and yet he who offered them, offered you the thing that you refused, as truly as the thing which you took. So God deceives no man, but with the Word and Sacrament He assuredly gives two things if they would take them. In His Word He offers the Word to the ear, He offers Christ Jesus to the soul; in His Sacraments, He offers the Sacraments to the eye, He offers Christ Jesus to the soul. Now it may be that where two things are truly and conjointly offered, a man may receive the one and refuse the other. He receives the one because he has an instrument to take it, and he refuses the other because he lacks an instrument. I hear the Word because I have an ear to hear it with; I receive the Sacrament because I have a mouth with which to receive it; but as to the thing which Word and Sacrament represent, I may refuse it because I have neither a mouth to take it, nor an eye to perceive it. Therefore the fault is not on God's part, but on my part. The wicked have the Body and Blood of Christ offered to them conjointly with the Word and Sacraments, but the fault is theirs for they do not have a mouth to take Him, and God is not bound to give them a mouth. Take note of that. And if it were not of His special grace and mercy that He gives me an eye to perceive Him, and a mouth to receive Him, I would refuse Him as well as they. So this argument does not hold either: Christ is offered to all, therefore He is received of all. Happy were they if they received Him. So much for the third argument.

The sacramental expressions

What remains now for the full understanding of the Sacrament? We have still to understand the sacramental expressions used in the Sacrament: the use we make of them, God's use in speaking them, and the use we think the Fathers made of them. We use them to say that the soul eats the Body of Christ and drinks the Blood of Christ. But this needs to be opened up and explained to you. When we speak about eating the Body and drinking the Blood of Christ, these expressions are sacramental. Eating and drinking, as you know, are the proper actions of the body only; but they are ascribed to the soul by a translation, by a figurative manner of speaking. That which is proper to the body is ascribed to the soul, and the soul is said to eat and drink. The eating of the soul must resemble the eating of the body. The eating of the soul is nothing else than the applying of Christ to the soul, believing that He has shed His Blood for me and has purchased remission of sins for me. But why do you call this an eating? Let us see what we mean by the eating of the body. When your body eats, you apply the meat to your mouth. If then the eating of the body is nothing else than the applying of meat to the mouth, the eating of the soul must be nothing else than the applying of the nourishment to the soul. So you see what is meant by the eating and drinking of the soul: nothing else than the applying of Christ, the applying of His death and passion to my soul. This is done only by faith, therefore he who lacks faith cannot eat Christ. So much for the eating and drinking of the soul, which is a sacramental way of speaking.

The application of Christ to the soul

Of all these great doctrinal things, there still remains one lesson to be learned—how to apply Christ rightly to your soul. Learn that and you have everything. If you have learned this well, you are a great theologian. For the right application of Christ to the sick soul, to the wounded conscience, and the diseased heart, is the fountain of all our felicity, and the well-spring of all our joy. In order to understand how this application operates (provided that you want Christ in your soul), think of what the presence of your soul within you does to this earthly body, to this lump of clay. It is by the presence of the soul that it lives, moves, and feels. As the soul gives to the body, life, movement, and sensation, so Christ does the very same thing to your soul. Have you ever grasped and applied Him to yourself? As the soul quickens the body, so He quickens the soul, not with an earthly or temporal life, but with the life which He lives in heaven. He makes you live the same life which the angels live in heaven. He makes you move, not with worldly motion, but with heavenly, spiritual and celestial motions. Again, He inspires in you not outward senses, but heavenly senses. He works within you a spiritual feeling, that in your own heart and conscience you may find the effect of His Word. Thus by the conjunction of Christ with my soul, I get a thousand times a greater benefit than the body does by the soul, for the body by the presence of the soul gets only an earthly and temporal life, subject to continual misery, but by the presence of Christ in my soul, I see a blessed life, I feel a blessed life, and that life daily increases in me more and more. Therefore the ground of all our perfection and blessedness consists in this conjunction and so even if you lived as long as Methuselah, and spent your whole life seeking, yet if in the last hour you were to get this conjunction, you would think your labour well worth it, for you would have gained enough. If you have gained Christ, you have gained everything with Him. Thus the applying of Christ to your soul is the fountain of all your joy and felicity.

Now let us see how we get this conjunction. This is a spiritual conjunction, hard and difficult to be acquired or procured. How then is it brought about? What are the means God uses in this conjunction, and what are the means man uses in it in order to get Christ, to put Christ Jesus in our soul, and to make Christ Jesus one with us? There is one means employed on God's part—God helps us to get Christ; and another means employed on our part. On the part of God, there is the Holy Spirit, who offers the Body and Blood of Christ to us. On our part there must also be a means employed, or else when He offers, we will not be able to receive. Therefore there must be faith in our souls to receive what the Holy Spirit offers, to receive the heavenly food of the Body and Blood of Christ. *Thus faith and the Holy Spirit are the two means employed in this spiritual and heavenly conjunction.* By these two means, by faith and the Holy Spirit, I receive the Body of Christ—the Body of Christ is mine, and He is given to my soul.

How is Christ in heaven given to us on earth?

A question arises here. How can you say that the Body of Christ is given or delivered to you, since the Body of Christ is sitting at the right hand of God the Father? See how great the distance is between heaven and earth—so great is the distance between the Body of Christ and your body. How then can you say that the Body of Christ is given to you? The Papists cannot understand this, and therefore they imagine a gross and carnal conjunction. Unless the Spirit of God reveals these things, they cannot be understood. The Spirit of God must enlighten our minds, and operate in all our hearts, before we can come to understand this.

Would you understand, then, how Christ is given to you? It is true that the Body of Christ is at the right hand of the Father, and that the Blood of Christ is at the right hand of the Father; nevertheless, although there is as great a distance between my body and the Body of Christ as there is between heaven and earth, Christ's Body is really given to me. He is given to me because His title is given to me; it is because the right and title to His Body and Blood is given to me that I am made to possess His Body and Blood. The distance of place does not hurt my title or my right. If any of you has a piece of land lying in the farthest part of Orkney, if you have a good title to it, the distance of place cannot hurt it. Likewise,

the distance of place does not hurt my title and my right
that I have to Christ. Even if He is sitting at the right
hand of the Father, yet the title and right that I have
make Him mine, so that I may truly say that He is my
property. Christ is not made mine because I pluck Him
out of the heavens, but He is mine because I have a sure
title and right to Him, and since I have a sure title and a
just right to Him, no distance, however great it may be,
can make any difference to my possession of Him.
Moreover, the title which I do have to Him is confirmed
to me for since I get my title to Him in the Word, so in
the Sacrament I get the confirmation of my title. If I got
no title to Him in the Word, I would not dare come to
the Sacrament; but now in the Sacrament I receive the
seal which confirms the title to Him I was given in the
Word.

Christ's Body, then, sits at the right hand of the
Father, and yet He is mine, and is delivered to me
because I have the right to His Body wherever it may be.
He was born for me, given to me, and delivered to me.
Therefore distance of place does not hurt, and nearness
of place does not help, the certainty of my title. Even if
Christ should bow the heavens, and touch you with His
Body, as He did Judas, yet this could not help you at all,
for if you had no title to Him, you could not call Him
yours. Thus it is not nearness or proximity of place that
makes Christ mine; it is only the right that I have to
Him. I have right to Him only through faith; therefore
by faith alone, Christ is made mine.

The Papists think that they have gained a great
advantage over us if we are as far from Christ as the
heaven is from the earth; but this advantage shall be
taken from them also, by God's grace. I have a title to
His Body but though His Body is distant from my body,

yet His Body is not distant from me, that is, from my soul. His body and my soul are conjoined. That is a strange ladder that stretches between heaven and earth, but I have a cord that goes from heaven to earth and couples me and Christ together, that is the cord of true faith. Even if Christ is in the heavens, He is coupled and conjoined with me on earth by true faith. How can this be? Let me show you. Is not the body of the Sun in the heavens? It is impossible for you to touch the body of the Sun, and yet the body of the Sun and you are conjoined by the beams and by the light that shine on you. Why then may not the Body of Christ, although it is in the heavens, be conjoined with me here upon earth, through the beams, by the light and gladness that flow from His Body? My body and the Body of Christ are conjoined by the virtue and power that flow from His Body; virtue and power which quicken my dead soul, make me live the life of Christ, and begin to die to myself; and the more I die to myself, the more I live to Him. This conjunction is the ground of all our felicity and happiness, as I have tried to explain to you, as clearly as I can.

This conjunction between our body and the Body of Christ is brought about by two special means: by means of the Holy Spirit, and by means of faith. But if there is no other means than these two, why do you require carnal or a visible conjunction? Faith is invisible, and the Spirit is invisible. You cannot see it, or perceive it with the eye of your body; the power of the Holy Spirit is so imperceptible, secret and invisible that you cannot perceive it or apprehend it with the eye of your body. And yet He produces great effects in your soul without your being able to perceive His operation. Therefore because the agencies of this conjunction are so imperceptible, secret and spiritual, why do you think you can see this conjunction with the eye of your body? Why do you imagine such a carnal conjunction as this, and which would not do you any good, even if you did see it? Do you not know that the Spirit who joins us and Christ is infinite, so that it is as easy for the Spirit to join Christ and us, no matter how distant we may be, as it is for our soul to link our head and the feet of our body, though they are separated from one another?

'You must be born again'

Therefore, seeing this conjunction is the ground and fountain of all our happiness, and seeing this ground of happiness is so imperceptible and spiritual, what is your part in it? Remove all your outward senses, all your natural notions, your natural discourses, and your natural reason, and follow the sight and information of the Spirit of God. Pray that it may please Him to enlighten your understanding, that by the light of His Spirit you may see the spiritual conjunction clearly. Unless the eye of the Spirit is given to you, to apprehend this spiritual conjunction, it is not possible for you to get any insight regarding it; but if the Lord in His mercy bestows some measure of His Holy Spirit upon you, then without doubt you will soon come to understand it, and you will be glad of the day when you heard the Word. Apart from a gift of the Spirit, it is not possible for you to be spiritual. That which is born of flesh and blood must remain flesh and blood, unless the Spirit comes in and makes it spiritual. Therefore you must be born again of the Spirit; you must be born in the Body of Christ, and His Spirit must quicken you. This is called by John the quickening and living Spirit of Christ. What does this Spirit do as soon as He comes into us? He

95

chases away darkness out of our understanding. Whereas before I knew not God, now I see Him, not only with a general knowledge that He is God, but I know that He is God in Christ. What else does the Holy Spirit do? He opens the heart as well as the mind. Those things on which I bestowed the affection of my heart, and employed the love of my soul, are now, by the working of the Holy Spirit, made gall to me. He makes me hate them as much as poison. He produces such an inward disposition in my soul that He makes me turn and flee from the very thing on which I poured out my love before, and instead to pour it out upon God. This is a great perfection, but nevertheless, in some measure He makes me love God better than anything else. He changes the affections of my soul. He changes their faculties and qualities. But although the substance of our hearts and minds is not changed they are made new to such an extent that we are called new creatures. Unless we are new creatures, we are not in Christ.

This secret conjunction, then, is brought about by faith and by the Holy Spirit. By faith we lay hold upon the Body and Blood of Christ, and though we are as far distant as heaven and earth are, the Spirit serves as a ladder to conjoin us with Christ, like the ladder of Jacob, which reached from the ground to the heavens. So the Spirit of God conjoins the Body of Christ with my soul. In a word, then, what is it that gives you any right or title to Christ? Nothing but the Spirit, nothing but faith. What are you to do then? By all means, try to get faith, so that as Peter says (Acts 15:9) your hearts and consciences may be sanctified by faith. If you do not seek to get faith in your hearts as well as in your minds, your faith will not avail. What does faith avail which only floats in the imagination, and brings a naked knowledge without opening up the heart, and involving the consent of the will. So there must be an opening of your heart, and a consent of your will, to do what God bids you do, or else your faith is of no avail. Then seek to get faith in your heart and mind, and in so doing, you do what Christians should do. This is not done without the diligent hearing of the Word, and diligent receiving of the Sacraments. Therefore be diligent in these exercises, and be diligent in prayer, praying in the Holy Spirit that He may nourish your souls inwardly with the Body and Blood of Christ, that He may increase faith in your hearts and minds, and make it grow up daily more and more, until you come to the full fruition of that blessed immortality. To this may the Lord in His mercy bring us, for the righteous merits of Christ Jesus, to whom with the Father and the Holy Spirit be all honour, praise and glory, both now and for ever. Amen.

3

THE LORD'S SUPPER
IN PARTICULAR 2

For I have received of the Lord that which also I delivered
unto you, that the Lord Jesus, the night in which He was
betrayed, took bread...

I CORINTHIANS 11:23.

DEARLY beloved in Christ Jesus, we heard in our last lesson what names were given to the Sacrament of the Supper, both in God's Book, and by the Fathers of the Latin and Eastern Churches. We heard the principal ends for which this holy Sacrament was instituted. We heard about the things contained in the Sacrament, what they were, how they are conjoined, how they are delivered, and how they are received. We heard also some objections that might be levelled against this doctrine; we heard them propounded and as God gave the grace, refuted; and finally we heard how the faithful soul is said to eat Christ's Body, and drink His Blood. We heard how Christ is, or can be, received by us, and we concluded with this: that Christ Jesus, the Saviour of mankind, our Saviour, cannot be perceived or received except in a spiritual way, and by spiritual apprehension. The Flesh and the Blood of Christ, or Christ Himself, cannot be perceived, except by the eye of faith, or be received, except by the mouth of faith; nor He be laid hold of, except by the hand of faith. Now, faith is a spiritual thing, for faith, is the gift of God, sent down into the hearts and minds of men, and wrought in their souls by the mighty working and operation of the Holy Spirit. Thus, since the only way to lay hold on Christ is by faith, and since faith by its very nature is spiritual, it follows that there is no way to lay hold on Christ except a spiritual way. There is no hand to grasp Christ but a spiritual hand, no mouth to feed on Him, but a spiritual mouth. In these familiar terms the Scriptures indicate the nature and efficacy of faith.

In the Sacrament, we are said to eat the Flesh of Christ and to drink His Blood by faith, chiefly by doing two things. *First, we call to our remembrance the bitter death and passion of Christ*, the Blood which He shed on the Cross, the Supper which He instituted in remembrance of Him before He went to the Cross, the commandment which He gave, 'Do this in remembrance of me'. We eat His Flesh and drink His Blood spiritually, primarily in recording and remembering faithfully how He died for us, how His Blood was shed on the Cross. This is the first point which cannot be remembered truly unless it is wrought by the mighty power of the Holy Spirit. *Secondly, spiritual eating consists in this: that I, and every one of you believe firmly that He died for me in particular*, that His Blood was shed on the Cross for a full remission and redemption of me and my sins. The chief principal thing in the eating of Christ's Flesh and drinking of His Blood consists in believing firmly that His Flesh was delivered to death for my sins, that His Blood was shed for the remission of my sins. Unless every soul draws near to Christ Himself, and firmly consents, agrees and is persuaded that Christ died for him, he cannot be saved, and cannot eat the Flesh or drink the Blood of Christ. Thus the eating of the Flesh and drinking of the Blood of Christ consists in a faithful memory in a firm belief and in a true applying of the merits of the death and passion of Christ to my own conscience in particular.

Various objections have been levelled against this kind of reception, which I will not repeat to you. Among them you have heard this objection against the spiritual perception of Christ by faith: 'If Christ's Flesh and Blood are not perceived or received except by the spirit or by faith, then,' they say, 'you receive Him only by your imagination. If He is not received carnally, or corporally, but only by the Spirit and by faith, then He is not received at all, except by way of imagination, thought and fancy.' Thus they account faith and imagination of the mind, a fantasy and an opinion, floating about in the brains of men. I cannot blame them for thinking like that about faith, for as no one can judge the sweetness of honey unless he has tasted it, so no one can judge the nature of faith except he who has felt and tasted it in his heart.

If they had tasted and felt in their souls what faith brings with it, they would not, alas, call that spiritual jewel—the only jewel of the soul—an imagination. They call it an imagination, but the Apostle describing it in Hebrews 11:1, calls it a substance, and a substantial ground. See how well these two agree: an imagination, and a substantial ground! They call it an uncertain opinion, floating about in the brain and imagination of man; the Apostle calls it an evidence and demonstration in the same definition. See how directly contrary to each other they and the Apostle are in regard to the nature of faith. They infer a general truth, that Christ cannot be delivered or given except in the same way that He is received. 'Observe how anything is received,' they say. 'It is given and delivered in the same way. Thus, if Christ is received by way of the imagination, He is also,' they imagine, 'given and delivered by way of the imagination.' If He is not given to your hand, to your mouth, or to the corporal stomach, then He cannot be given except through the imagination or fantasy. The reason why they think that Christ cannot be theirs or be given to them truly, in actuality and reality, unless He is given carnally, is this: that which is as far away and as distant from us as the heaven is from the earth, cannot be said to be given to us, or to be ours. 'By your own confession,' they say to us, 'Christ's Body is as far away from us as the heaven is from the earth; therefore Christ's Flesh cannot be given to us, and so not truly or in actuality.'

We on earth have a 'title' to Christ who is in heaven

Put in this way, their argument would seem at first sight to have some force, but let us examine it. The proposition is this: that which is as far away from us as the heaven is from the earth, cannot be said to be delivered to us, to be given to us, or in any way to be ours. Now, is this proposition true or false? I say that it is quite false, and that the contrary is most true. A thing may be given to us and may become ours although the thing itself is as distant from us as the heaven is from the earth. How can I prove this? What makes anything yours? What makes any of you count that something is given to you? Is it not a title, is it not a just right to that thing? If you have a just right given to you by Him who has the power to give it, and a sure title granted to you by Him who has the power to do so, even if the thing that He gives you is not delivered into your hands, yet by the right and title which He grants to you, is not the thing yours? There can be no question about it, for it is not the nearness of a thing to my body and to my hand that makes it mine. It may be in my hand, and yet not belong to me. Neither is it the distance, or the absence of a thing, that makes it mine; for it may be far away from me, and yet be mine, because the title is mine, and because I have got a right to it from Him who has the power to give it. So then this is a true principle: what makes a thing ours is a sure title and a just right to it, even if it is absent, or far away from us. We take it for granted, therefore, that a lively and true faith in the Blood and death of Christ gives us a sure title and a good right to the Flesh and Blood of Christ, and to His merits.

Consider what He merited by His death and the shedding of His Blood upon the Cross—all that together with Himself belongs to me, by a title and a right to Him which I have got from God, which is faith. And the surer my title is, the surer I am of the thing that is given to me by the title.

Our title to Christ is confirmed by the Lord's Supper

Now this Sacrament of the Lord's Supper was instituted to confirm our title, to seal our right, which we have to the Body and Blood, to the death and passion of Christ. And so the Body of Christ is said to be given to us, the Blood of Christ is said to be delivered to us, when our title to Him, to His death and to His Body and Blood, is confirmed in our hearts. This Sacrament is instituted for the growth and increase of our faith, for the increase of our holiness and sanctification. The greater this faith is in our hearts, the more sure we are that Christ's death pertains to us. I grant, as I have said, that the Flesh of Christ is not delivered into my hands, or put into my mouth; nor does it enter into my stomach, but God forbid that you should say He is not truly given.

Why should Christ's Flesh be put into your hand, or into the mouth of your body? Has He not appointed bread and wine for the nourishment of the body, and can you not be content with that? Are they not sufficient to nourish you for this earthly and temporal life? It is Christ whom He has appointed to be delivered to the inward mouth of your soul, to be given into the hand of your soul, that your soul may feed on Him, and be quickened with the very life which the angels live, which the Son of God and God Himself live. Thus the Flesh of Christ is not appointed to nourish your body, but to nourish your soul, in the hope and in the growth of that immortal life.

Therefore, even if the Flesh of Christ is not delivered into the hands of your body, it is delivered to that part of you which it is meant to nourish, that is, to the soul. Indeed, the bread and the wine are delivered to the hand and mouth of your body, not more really than the Flesh of Christ is delivered to the hand and mouth of your soul, which is faith. Therefore yearn no more for a carnal delivery, and do not think further of any carnal reception of Christ. You must not think that God gives the Flesh of Christ to the mouth of your body, or that by the mouth of your body you receive the Flesh of Christ. You must understand this principle of the Scriptures of God: our souls cannot be joined or united with the Flesh of Christ, nor can the Flesh of Christ be joined to our souls, except by a spiritual bond—not by a carnal bond or alliance of blood, nor by the contact of His Flesh with our flesh. He is conjoined with us by a spiritual bond, that is, by the power and virtue of the Holy Spirit, and therefore the Apostle says in 1 Corinthians 12:13, that by means of His Holy Spirit all we who are faithful men and women are baptised into the one Body of Christ, that is we are conjoined and bound together with one Christ by means of one Spirit, not by a carnal bond or by any gross conjunction, but only by the bond of the Holy Spirit.

The Spirit's work in the Sacrament of the Lord's Supper

The same Holy Spirit who is in Him is in every one of us in some measure, and because one Spirit is in Him and in us, therefore we are all reckoned to be one Body and to be members of one spiritual and mystical Body. In the same verse the Apostle says 'we are all made to drink into one and the selfsame Spirit', that is, we are made to drink of the Blood of Christ, and this Blood is nothing else than the quickening virtue and power that flow from Christ and from the merits of His death. We are all made to drink of that Blood when we drink of the lively power and virtue that flow from His Blood. Thus the only bond which can bind my soul to the Flesh of Christ is a spiritual bond, or a spiritual union. Therefore, the Apostle says, 'He that is joined to the Lord is one Spirit' (1 Cor. 6:17), and John says (3:6), 'That which is born of the Spirit is spirit.' It is then only by the participation of the Holy Spirit that we are conjoined with the Flesh and Blood of Christ Jesus. The carnal bond, whether it be the bond of blood running through one race, or the carnal contact of flesh with flesh, was never esteemed by Christ. When He lived here upon the earth, He thought nothing of that bond, and as we read in the Scriptures which He has given to us, He did not respect or esteem it in comparison with the spiritual bond. This spiritual bond, however, through which we are united to Him by one Spirit, He ever esteemed while He lived on earth, and He has left us in the Scriptures praise and commendation of it.

To show you how lightly He estimated the carnal bond of blood and kindred which we regard so highly, consider this passage from Luke 8:20 and 21. When people came to Him and said 'Master, thy mother and thy brethren stand without, and would see thee', His answer shows how little He esteemed the carnal bond. In the 21st verse He answers in a way which denies the bond, when He says: 'My mother and my brethren are these which hear the Word of God, and do it.' It is as if He would say, it is not the carnal conjunction that I esteem and reverence, but the spiritual conjunction, by the participation of the Holy Spirit, through which we are moved to hear the Word of God, to reverence and obey it. This carnal bond was never profitable, as the same passage in Luke 8 plainly testifies. If the contact of Christ's Flesh had been profitable, the multitude mentioned in the chapter that thrust and pressed upon Him, had been the better for its carnal contact. Not one of them, therefore, was the better for the carnal contact, therefore it profits nothing. And so Christ Himself says in John 6:63, in order to draw them away from that strange confidence in His flesh, 'The flesh profits nothing, it is the Spirit that quickens.'

Illustration of the woman who touched Christ in faith

As to the other kind of touch, contact by the Holy Spirit and by faith in your soul, this has always been profitable, and we have a clear illustration of it in the same chapter (Luke 8:43-48). Thus the poor woman who had long been diseased with an issue of blood for the space of twelve years, and had wasted and consumed a great part of her substance in seeking a cure for it, found no help in the natural and bodily physicians. At last by virtue of the Holy Spirit working faith in her heart, by faith she understands and realises that she is able to recover the health of her body, and the health of her soul, by Christ Jesus, who came to save both body and soul. With this persuasion in her heart that Christ could cure both body and soul, she came to Him, and as the text says, she pressed through the multitude until she came to Him; and when she came to Him, it is not said that she touched His Flesh with her hand (in case the Papists would ascribe the virtue which came out of Him to her carnal touching) but it is said that she touched only the hem of His garment with her hand, and with faith, which is the hand of the soul, she touched her Saviour, God and Man. And to show you that she touched Him by faith, Jesus said to her in the end, 'Go thy way, thy faith hath saved thee'.

She no sooner touched Him by faith than immediately there came power out of Him. She felt the power and virtue by its effects in her soul, and our Saviour felt it when it went out of Him. As soon as He felt it, He said 'Who touched me?' Peter (who was always most impetuous) said 'Thou seest the multitude thronging thee, and sayest thou Who touched me?' Our Saviour answered again, 'It is not that touching I am speaking of, but another kind of touching: someone has touched me who has drawn a virtue and power out of me. The multitude does not take virtue from me like that.' The poor woman, thinking she had done amiss, and seeing that she could not be hid, came trembling and said: 'I did it.' He answered her in the end, and said: 'Depart in peace, thy faith hath saved thee.' 'Thy faith hath drawn out a virtue and power from me that has made you whole, both in soul and body.'

This touching of Christ has always been profitable. It still is, and always will be profitable, unlike the touching of Christ with the corporal hand. Why? Christ is not appointed to be a carnal [physical] head, to be set upon the necks of our bodies, to provide our bodies with natural senses and motions. No, the Scriptures do not call Christ a natural head, but they call Him a spiritual Head to be set upon the necks of our souls, that is to be conjoined with our souls, that out of Him there may distill into our souls holy motions and heavenly senses, and that there may flow out of Him into us a spiritual and heavenly life. Therefore the Scriptures call Him a spiritual Head, as they call us a spiritual Body.

As the life which we get from Him is spiritual, so all our conjunction with Him is spiritual. And because He works the same operation in the soul which the carnal head does in the body, He is said to be a spiritual Head. Therefore He is counted the Head of His Church, because He provides her with spiritual motion and senses, which is the life of the Church.

To be brief, then, there is nothing carnal [physical] in this conjunction, there is nothing gross in it, there is nothing to be grasped by our natural judgements and understanding. Therefore whoever would attain the smallest insight into the spiritual conjunction between Christ and us, must of necessity humble himself and earnestly pray for the Spirit, otherwise it is not possible to get any understanding even if it be ever so slight, of how the Flesh of Christ and we are conjoined, unless we have some light given to us by the Spirit, that is, unless our hearts are awakened by the mighty working of the Spirit of Christ, this will remain as a dead and closed letter to us.

The frame of mind in which to come to the Lord's Table

Firstly, you should pray, therefore, that the Lord in His mercy may awaken you, enlighten your understanding, and give you a spiritual light in which to discern spiritual things. *Secondly*, you should endeavour to remove all vain cogitations and earthly fantasies. When you come to hear of so high a matter, you must cast off all filthy thoughts, evil desires, and cares of the world, and everything that clogs your heart. And *thirdly*, you must come intending to hear the Word, to give diligent ear to the Word, and to receive it with a sanctified heart. You must desire to grow and increase in holiness, in soul as well as in body, all the days of your life. And when you come like that, unquestionably the Holy Spirit will reveal those things to you which you need. Even if this Word you are hearing passes, and brings no great benefit at the time, yet afterwards the Holy Spirit will reveal to you the truth of what you have now heard. This then is the important point: be present with your heart and mind, and let your souls be emptied of all the cares of the world, that they may receive the wine which is offered in the hearing of the Word.

The definition of the Sacrament of the Lord's Supper

Now I come to the definition of the Sacrament of the Lord's Supper. *I call the Sacrament a holy seal, annexed to the Covenant of grace and mercy in Christ.* It is a seal to be administered publicly, according to the holy institution of Christ Jesus, that in its lawful administration the sacramental union between the sign and the thing signified, may take place. In this union Christ Jesus, who is the thing signified, is as truly delivered to the increase of our spiritual nourishment as the signs are given and delivered to the body for our temporal nourishment.

Now let us examine the terms and parts of this definition. *First of all*, I call the Sacrament the *seal* because it serves the same purpose for our souls as a common seal serves for a common document. As a seal which is annexed to the document confirms and seals up the truth contained in it, so the Sacrament of the Body and Blood of Christ confirms and seals up the truth of mercy and grace contained in the Covenant of mercy and grace. That is why it is called a seal.

Secondly, it is called a *holy seal*: Why? because it is taken from the common use to which the bread, for example, was put the night before, and is now applied to a holy use. A power is given to the bread to signify the precious Body of Christ Jesus, to represent the nourishing and feeding of our souls. Because now in the Sacrament it is applied to such a holy use, I call it a holy seal. This is not my word, it is the word of the Apostle, who in Romans 4:11 gives the Sacrament the same name when he calls it a seal. If the wisdom of Christ in His Apostle had been followed, and if men had not invented new names of their own for the Sacrament, but had contented and satisfied themselves with the names which God had given by His Apostle, and which Christ Himself had given to this Sacrament, I am sure that none of these dissensions, none of these great storms and endless debates would have happened. Where men insist on being wiser than God, and go beyond God in devising on their own names which He never gave, such dissensions and debates take place. This teaches us, by the way, that no flesh should presume to be wiser than God. Let us rather condescend to keep the name which God has given to the Sacrament.

Thirdly, the Sacrament is annexed to the *Covenant,* annexed and attached to the Charter. It cannot properly be called a seal, unless it is attached to a document. By itself a seal remains what it is by nature, and is nothing more than that unless it is annexed to some document. It is only its attachment to a document that makes men account it a seal. Thus it is not esteemed at all unless it is attached to the document. So it is here. *If this Sacrament is not administered in conjunction with the preached Word, and joined to the preaching of the Covenant of mercy and grace, it cannot be a seal.* It is no more than what it is by nature, it is only a common piece of bread, and nothing more, unless it is annexed to the preaching of the Word and administered along with it, as Christ has commanded. Therefore I say the seal must be annexed, appended and joined to the documentary evidence, to the preaching of the Word, in confirmation of it, otherwise it is not a seal. However, with the documentary evidence which is the Word of God, it is somewhat different, for as you know, any document will produce faith and establish a right even if it is subscribed without a seal; but the seal without the document is of no value at all. So it is with the Word of God. Even if the Sacrament is not annexed to the Word, yet the Word will do its work: it enables us to receive Christ; it serves to engender and beget faith in us, and makes us grow up in faith. But the seal without the Word can not serve us in any holy use. Therefore the seal must be annexed to the Word preached, to the Covenant of mercy and grace.

Communion to be administered publicly

Now it follows from the definition that this seal must be administered publicly. Why publicly? *First,* to exclude all private administration of the Sacrament. If the Sacrament is administered to anyone privately, it is not a Sacrament, because the Apostle calls this Sacrament a *Communion*; therefore if you administer it to one person alone, you lose the Sacrament. This Sacrament is a Communion of the Body and Blood of Christ, and therefore of necessity it must be by way of communication, and so the action must be publicly administered.

Secondly, this Sacrament must be *publicly* administered because Christ Jesus, who is the thing signified in the Sacrament, does not belong to one man only. If this were so, He might be privately given, and ministered. But since Christ, who is the thing signified in the Sacrament, belongs to every believing man, every faithful man and woman, therefore He ought to be given in common to all, in a common action, in a fellowship in congregation of the faithful.

Thirdly, this Sacrament is called a *Thanksgiving* to God the Father for His benefits. Now it does not pertain to one or two only to thank God; we are all partakers of His temporal and spiritual benefits; therefore we all ought publicly to give Him thanks for them. That is why I said in the definition that this seal ought to be administered publicly and not privately, as the Papists do in their private masses.

The Sacrament a divine institution and command

This seal must be publicly administered according to Christ's institution. Why do we keep to Christ's institution, rather than man's or angel's institution? Because neither man nor angel has power to institute or make a Sacrament. No one has this power except He who has power to give Christ, who is the thing signified in the Sacrament; but no one has power to give Christ except the Father or Christ Himself, therefore no one has power to make or institute a Sacrament except either the Father or the Son. Only God may make a Sacrament. Further, this Sacrament is a part of God's service and worship, but no one has power to appoint any part of His service or prescribe any part of His worship except God Himself, therefore no one can make a Sacrament but God alone. No Prince on earth will be content to be served according to another man's fantasy. He will prescribe his services according to his own pleasure. How much more fitting it is that God should appoint His own service and worship. Therefore no man or angel has power to institute any part of the service of God. The greatest title that any man on earth may be given in the ministry of the Word and Sacrament, is the title which the Apostle gives in I Corinthians 4:1. There we are called stewards and dispensers of the graces of God, ministers of the mysteries and holy things. It follows from this that we are not authors, creators, or makers of them, but only ministers and dispensers of the Sacrament. It is clear then that no man or creature has power to make a Sacrament; therefore it must be according to the institution of Christ. Consider what He said, what He did, and what He commanded you to do; all that must be said, done and obeyed.

It is His institution that must be kept. If you leave undone one jot of what He commanded you to do, you pervert the institution, for there is nothing in the register of the institution but what is essential. Thus in the celebration of Christ's institution, we must pay attention to whatever He said, did or commanded to be done. We must first say whatever He said, and then do whatever He did, for the administration of the Sacrament must follow upon the Word. You must first teach what Christ commanded you to teach, and then administer the Sacrament faithfully keeping to this institution.

Now the Word of the Sacrament I call the whole institution of Christ Jesus, preached and proclaimed, expounded distinctly, clearly and sensibly to the people. Thus if we leave any particular point or ceremony belonging to this institution undone, we pervert the whole action. It is agreed and accepted between us who celebrate this institution and all the sects of the world who have separated themselves from this institution, that two things are necessary, and must combine in the nature and constitution of the Sacrament, namely there must be a Word and there must be an Element combined with it. There is not a sect but grants this, that the Word must be added to the Element before there can be a Sacrament.

Although they easily admit this in general, in which we agree with them, yet when it comes down to particulars, in the actual handling and treating of the Word, we are very far removed from them. However much we appear to agree with them in general, we are poles apart when we come to discuss and reason about these particular five points:—

[1] What is meant by the Word,

[2] How this Word is to be treated,

[3] What virtue this Word has,

[4] How far the virtue of this Word extends,

[5] To whom the words are to be directed and declared.

1. What is meant by the Word

I will leave the other sects alone, and deal only with the Papists, because we have most to do with them. First of all we must understand what *we* mean by the Word, and what *they* mean by the Word. *By the Word we understand the whole institution of Christ Jesus, whatever He said or did or commanded to be done, without addition or subtraction, without any alteration in the meaning or sense of the Word.* This is what we mean by the Word in the Sacrament.

Now what do the Papists understand by the Word? They do not preach the institution of Christ, or take the whole institution as He left it, but instead they select and pick out of His institution four or five words, and they make the whole virtue of the institution consist in them. That would not matter so much if they would content themselves with these words, because they are the words of the institution, but they add to the words, they subtract from them, and they alter their meaning at their pleasure. In order that you may understand this in their Mass, as they call the Supper, I shall explain it to you. I shall divide the Mass into what is substantial and what is accidental. They hold that to the substance of the Mass three things are necessary. *First,* there must of necessity be a priest, that is to say, one who takes upon himself the office of our Mediator, Christ Jesus, to intercede between God and man. *Secondly,* it is required that the priest offer the Body and Blood of Christ. We come here to receive these things, but the priest offers them to God the Father. *Thirdly,* by this work (they say) they obtain all good things; by this work wrought they obtain remission of sins for the dead as well as for the living, but especially for the priest himself who is the distributor and for him to whom the priest applies that

Sacrament. As for the rest of the Church, who are absent, they obtain remission of their sins by this work generally. These three things are necessary to the substance of the Mass.

As for the accidents[1] that go to the making of a Mass, they are of two sorts: some of them are always necessary, without which that action cannot take place; some are not necessary, on the other hand, and the action may take place without them, but not without a deadly sin. These things that are necessary partly concern the priest, and partly concern the action itself. The accidents necessary to the priest are of two sorts: one sort are those without which he cannot be a priest, the other sort, those without which he cannot be free of deadly sin. The things without which he cannot be a priest are these: 1. power to consecrate, given by his Bishop, which is given to him by the unction and the shaving of the crown of his head; and 2. the power to speak, and therefore the roof of his mouth must be whole, so that he can speak. These two things which refer to his person are always necessary. Other things again are not so necessary, as: the priest must be free from suspension, from cursing, deadly sin, and all ecclesiastical punishment and censure. On the other hand, there are two things necessary to the action: one sort without which the action cannot take place, such as the Lord's Prayer, or the five Words of the Institution; other things again are not so necessary, such as the consecration of the place where the Mass is said, the

---

[1] 'Accident' in this context means 'a property not essential to our human conception of a substance', and thus can apply to the material qualities of bread and wine after transubstantiation is held to have taken place. See also explanation of 'accidents' on p. 127.

altar stone, the blessing of the chalice, the water, the mutterings, the singing, the assistant at the Mass, and the rest. Thus they and we in no way agree as concerning the Word and what is meant by it.

2. How the Word ought to be treated

We are just as far apart in regard to the second point, namely, how this Word ought to be treated. We say that the Word which concerns the whole institution ought to be treated in this way. *First*, there ought to be a lawful pastor , who has his calling from God to deliver it, and he ought to deliver the Word lawfully, that is, he ought to preach it, proclaim it, and announce it publicly with a clear voice. He ought to open it up, expound it in all its parts, declaring what is the people's part, what is his own part, declaring how he ought to deliver and distribute the bread and wine, and how the people ought to receive the bread and wine at his hands. He ought to inform their faith as to how they are to receive the Body and Blood of Christ signified by the bread and the wine. Moreover, he ought to teach them how they should come with great reverence to the Table and communicate with the precious Body and Blood of Christ. This he ought to do in familiar language, that the people may understand and hear him, that they may perceive and take up in their hearts the things he speaks. For what good is it to hear something whispered and not spoken out, or if it is spoken out, what does it avail if it is not understood? Unless you hear Christ in a familiar and homely language, you cannot understand, and unless you understand, it is not possible for you to believe. Without belief there is no application of Christ, and unless you believe and apply Christ to yourself, your coming to the Sacrament is in vain. Therefore, if this

Sacrament is to be lawfully handled, the pastor must preach the institution of Christ in such a way that it is heard and in a familiar language, that it may be understood. He must preach it in such a way that faithful people may be informed how they are to receive it, and the Minister may know his own part in delivering and distributing the bread and wine. This we say should be the proper handling of the holy institution of the Sacrament.

Now, what do the Papists do? In place of a Minister, Pastor or Bishop (call him what you please), who is lawfully called of God, they substitute a priest, putting in his place a hireling who has no calling or office in the Church of God. For the office of a priest, in their sense of the priesthood, is nothing else than the office of Christ Jesus, the office of the Mediator between God and us. They make their priests daily to offer up Christ Jesus to the Father, but this is the office of the Mediator, and Christ did it once for ever and for all of us, as the Apostle says, so that there is no possibility for them to do this over again. When therefore their priests presume to do this again, which Christ has done already, they do it without command, they have no warrant for it in the Word of God. But even if they had a warrant for their calling in the Word of God, yet they handle the Sacrament wrongly, for where they ought to speak out clearly, they whisper, and conjure the Elements by some kind of muttering: where they should speak it in a known language, that the people may understand, they speak it in an unknown language; and even if they did speak it in a known and familiar language, yet because they whisper it, the people cannot benefit by it. What shall I say, then, when they handle the Word in this way? Even if it be the very institution itself, they so spoil

117

it in their handling of it, that it is not a holy Sacrament. Thus we differ as much in the second point, namely how the Word ought to be handled and treated.

3. The virtue the Word of God has

Now we come to the third point—namely, what virtue this Word has and how far the virtue of this Word extends itself. We grant and acknowledge that the Word has a virtue, and the Word in its appointment, as we have said, has a work to do, even with the elements of bread and wine. We acknowledge that these elements, by virtue of this Word, are changed, not in their substance, not in their nature, nor even in their substantial and natural properties, but we grant that the elements are changed in a quality which they had before, in such a way that these elements are taken from a common use which they served before, and by the institution of Christ, are now applied to a holy use. Note how far this holy use differs from the common use—there is as great a difference between the elements this day in the action and what they were yesterday. I grant that the elements are changed, but this change does not proceed from the nature of the elements, from some virtue supposed to be enclosed in the words, nor from the whispering of the words, but it proceeds from the will of Christ, from His ordinance and appointment, set down in His own institution, for that is holy which God calls holy, and that is profane which God calls profane.

To understand how these signs are made holy, two things must be considered, *first*, who is he who makes them holy—God, angel or man? *Secondly*, whoever he is that makes them holy, by what means and in what way does he make them holy? Through the consideration of these two questions, we shall reach a proper estimate of the sanctification of the elements.

How the elements are made holy

In answer to the first question, we say that it is God alone who makes a thing that is common to be holy. By His will and ordinance, declared and set down in His Word, God has made the things that were common, by His appointment, to be holy. In answer to the question as to the way and means whereby they are made holy, we say it is the Word of God, the institution of Christ, the will of Christ declared in His institution, that makes them holy. For the preaching and exposition of the Word and institution of Christ shows us that God has made these things holy, and not only that He has made them holy, but it shows us a holy way in which they are to be used, in what place, at what time, with what heart, and to what end. Thus it is the will of Christ, declared in His institution, by which the things that were common before are now made holy.

There are two other things also which make the same elements holy, and these two are used in this institution, namely *prayer* and *thanksgiving*. They make the creatures of God holy for our use. If we receive the creatures of God like dumb animals, and do not thank Him for them, it is a sure token that they are not sanctified for our use.

By prayer we obtain grace and strength from God to use the creatures, and this whole action, holily and lawfully, as it should be. And therefore not only in this holy action should we begin with God, and with the invocation of His Name, but in all actions in the world we should begin in God's Name. Thus it is the will of

God, prayer and thanksgiving conjoined with the Elements that make them holy. All these three contained in the action of the Supper makes the seals holy, for besides the will of God, declared in His institution, in the Supper we use an invocation, and in this invocation we use a thanksgiving. Thus the elements are not made holy by the will of God only, but by the use of prayer and thanksgiving. These three are the only means and ways by which these things are sanctified.

'To bless' and 'to give thanks' are equivalents

To express and declare the sanctification of the elements, the evangelists and the apostle Paul use indifferently the words 'to bless' and 'to give thanks'. They are commonly used as equivalents: Mark and Paul use the word 'bless', Matthew and Luke use the word 'to give thanks', and all with one signification. Mark himself in the 14th chapter of his Gospel, verse 22, when speaking of the action of the Supper, uses the word 'to bless', and in the 23rd verse he uses the word 'to give thanks', and both with the same meaning. Thus the apostle, Christ Himself, and the evangelists use the words 'to bless' and 'to give thanks' indifferently to signify the sanctification and consecration of the elements. Unless these words are used as equivalents, it would be hard to get a good meaning out of the apostle's words when in 1 Corinthians 10:16 he says, 'The cup of blessing which we bless'. What does that mean? I take the words 'which we bless' to signify 'which we sanctify and prepare by blessing, thus 'to bless' and 'to give thanks' in the Lord's Supper signify nothing else than 'to sanctify'. If we take the words in any other sense, we fall into error. God is said to bless, and man is said to bless:

God is said to bless when He gives good things to His creatures, for His blessing is always effectual, and therefore He is said to bless when He gives good things; man, again, is said to bless, either privately or publicly, when he craves blessing at the hands of God for any man, when he blesses in the Name and at the command of God, any person or people. Now if you ascribe blessing in any of these two significations to the Cup, it is quite false, for we neither crave blessing for insensible Elements, nor do we bless them in the name of God. God gives good things to the sons of men, not to insensible creatures. Therefore we are compelled to use the word 'bless' in a third sense—*'the Cup which we bless' means 'which we sanctify and prepare by blessing'*. That is what we understand by the sanctification of the Elements.

The five words: 'For this is my body'

Now let us see how the Papists sanctify their elements, and what is the form of their consecration So far as I understand, it consists in these five words: *hoc est enim corpus meum.* ('For this is my body'). It consists in the whispering of these five words, for if you do not whisper them, you lose the form of incantation; for what we call sanctifying, they call whispering, and the whispering of these five words they call the consecration of the elements. When the words are whispered in this way, they presuppose such a hidden and amazing virtue to be enclosed in the syllables that the virtue or power which flows from the words is able to chase away wholly the substance of the bread, so that the very bread, and substance of it, is altogether destroyed by this power. Moreover, this power that flows from these words is able to procure and draw down another substance, namely the Flesh and Blood of Christ Jesus, who sits at the right hand of His Father and is able to enclose it within the bread. This is a strange and a great virtue, that not only draws down that substance, but encompasses it within the bread! These same five words, whispered in this way, have such a wondrous operation, they say, that they are able both to do away with one substance, and to bring down the other, and to put it within the bread.

Now we altogether deny that there is such a virtue in these words. As I have said before, we do not deny that the Word has a virtue, but we deny that there is such a virtue enclosed in the words; we deny the quality of the virtue, and the quantity of the virtue, or that it flows from such a function. We grant indeed that the Word has a virtue, for there is no Word ever spoken by God but which has a virtue joined with it; but we deny that this virtue is enclosed in the syllables, in the whispering or pronouncing of the words. If there were such a virtue and power enclosed in the syllables, for the same reason it would follow that there is a virtue in the figure and shape of the letters that make up the words. Now no man thinks that there is any virtue in the figure or shape of the letter, and there is as little virtue in the syllables, or in the pronouncing of the words themselves. And so we deny that there is any virtue enclosed in the syllables, or resident in the words. But we say there is a power conjoined with the Word, and that this power is not resident in the words, but in the eternal Word, in the essential Word, of which John speaks in the first chapter of his Gospel. 'The Word which was from the beginning', that is, the Son of God, Christ Jesus. We say that there is not a dram weight of this virtue and power resident in any creature that ever God created, but it is only resident in Christ Jesus. Therefore there does not flow any virtue from the syllables, or from the words that are spoken, but from Christ and His Spirit, who gives the virtue to these words. This then is where we differ: we say that there is no virtue resident in the syllables, that the syllables and the pronouncing of them, work nothing; but we do say that the virtue is resident in the person of the Son of God, and He works by His own Word.

Now we say that there cannot be such an amazing change as that the whispering of so many words should change the proper substance of the bread, bring down the substance of the Body of Christ, and enclose His Body in such a narrow compass. We say that cannot be, and this I shall prove by three things, namely, by the reality of the Flesh of Christ Jesus, by the articles of our belief, and by the true end of the institution of the Sacrament. And so we shall see, by God's grace, the infinite absurdities that follow from the opinions of the Papists.

The first principle: the reality of the Flesh of Christ

The first principle that I lay down, is this —Christ Jesus, the Son of God, in the time appointed took true Flesh from the womb of the virgin, and united Himself with our nature, in a personal union, to the end that our nature, which fell altogether from its integrity in the first Adam, might recover the same in the second Adam—yes, not only the same, but much greater, as much as our second Adam in every way excels the first.

Therefore since He assumed a body like ours in all things (sin excepted) it must necessarily follow that the definition of a true body and its inseparable properties, must pertain to Him. But these are the inseparable properties, namely, to be in a certain place, to be circumscribed, visible and palpable; for all these belong (*quarto modo*, as the logicians say) to a body, so that they cannot be separated from the subject without its destruction. Therefore I reason in this way: every true human body is in a certain place; Christ Jesus' Body is a true human body; therefore it is in a certain place.

I call a place a certain condition of an organic body whereby it comes to pass that wherever the body is, it is of necessity limited within that place, and while it is there, it cannot be elsewhere. Do you require proof for my proposition from the doctors? Read Augustine's Epistle to Dardanus, where he speaks of this same Body of Christ. 'Take away a room or space from bodies, and they will be in no place, and if they are in no place, they are not.' This same Augustine in his thirtieth Homily on John's Gospel, says: 'The body in which the Lord rose again must of necessity be in one place, but His divine efficacy and nature is diffused everywhere.' And in his third Epistle he says: 'However big or however little the body may be, it must occupy a definite place.' And besides these, the history of the Acts proves most evidently that Christ's Body was in a certain place, as in Acts 3:21: 'Whom the heaven must contain until the time that all things do restore which God had spoken by the mouth of all his prophets.' Although I do not need to insist on proving these things, yet I proceed. Then I reason in this way: every human body is finite and circumscribed, but the Body of Christ is a human body. What warrant from the doctors do I have for this? I omit many on purpose and cite only from Augustine. Writing to Dardanus, he says: 'Believe Christ to be everywhere, in that He is God, but only to be in heaven, according to the nature of a true body.' And in his 146th Epistle, he says: 'I believe the Body of Christ so to be in heaven as it was on earth, when He went up to heaven.' But it was circumscribed in a certain place on earth, therefore it is so in heaven, and consequently it cannot both be in the bread of the Mass and in heaven at the same time.

The last reason is this: every human body is visible and palpable, but Christ has a human Body, and He is corporally present as you say. Therefore Christ's Body is visible and palpable. I prove my proposition by Christ's own words, taken from Luke 24:24, 39. In order to persuade the apostles of the reality of His Body, and to prove clearly that it was not a phantom, he uses the argument taken from these two qualities, and commands the apostles to feel and see, giving them thereby to understand that as these two senses are the most certain of all, so they are the most able to discern whether He was a body or a spirit, as if He would say, 'If I am visible and palpable, you may cease to doubt that I have a true body.' For as the poet says, whom Tertullian cites also for this same purpose:

Tangere enim et tangi, nisi corpus, nulla potest res.
('For nothing can touch or be touched except a body.')

By these arguments it may be clearly seen how transubstantiation is in no way consistent with the reality of the Body of Christ Jesus.

The second Principle: the articles of our Faith

As transubstantiation fights with the Flesh of Christ Jesus, so it is directly opposed to the articles of our Faith. For in our Belief we profess that Christ ascended from earth to heaven, where He sits at the right hand of the Father, where He governs and directs all things in heaven and earth, from which place He is to come at the

125

last day, to judge the world. This article teaches us that He has left His dwelling which He had amongst us on earth, and has ascended into heaven, where He sits at the right hand of His Father, and shall remain there, according to the testimony of Peter, which I cited from Acts 3:21, until the last day. If He sits at His Father's right hand and is to remain in heaven until the last day, He is not corporally in the bread. But the article says that He sits at the right hand of His Father, and Peter says in that place that He is to be contained in the heavens until the last day. Therefore this transubstantiation is directly opposed to the article of our Belief, and the plain teaching of the Scriptures.

The third principle: the true end of the Sacrament

Transubstantiation is opposed to the end for which this Sacrament was instituted. This is most evident, for the end of the Sacrament is spiritual, as the effect that flows from it is spiritual, and the instrument whereby the spiritual food is applied to us is also spiritual. But from a natural and corporal presence, a spiritual effect can never flow, Therefore the corporal and natural presence of the Body and Blood of Christ Jesus is directly opposed to the end of this Sacrament; for the corporal presence must have a corporal eating; of this eating there follows a digestion in the stomach, and the thing that is digested in the stomach can never feed your soul to life eternal. Thus the corporal presence must involve a corporal process, which is directly contrary to the end for which the Sacrament was instituted.

Moreover, if the bread were transubstantiated, it would become the thing signified. If it becomes the thing signified, this Sacrament would want a sign, and so it would not be a Sacrament, for every Sacrament, as you have heard, is a sign. Now to say that the accidents[2] of true bread, such as its colour and roundness, may serve as signs, is more than folly, for between the sign and the thing signified there must be a conformity, but there is no conformity between the accidents of the bread and wine, and the Body and Blood of Christ Jesus; for if that were so, the accidents ought to nourish us corporally, as the Body and Blood of Christ Jesus, are appointed to nourish us spiritually. Further, if the bread were to become the Body of Christ Jesus, it would follow that He had a Body without Blood, for He has instituted another sign to represent His Blood. Also, if there had been such a wonderful thing as they speak of in the Sacrament, there would have been plain mention of it in the Scripture; for God Himself never works a notable work but He declares it either openly, or privately, in the Scripture, that thereby He may be glorified in His wonderful works. So for example we may read in the Gospel of John 2:8 where the water is changed into wine; and Genesis 2:22, where the rib of Adam was changed into Eve; in Exodus 8:10, where Aaron's rod was turned into a serpent.

In all these instances the change is clearly expressed, therefore I say if there had been such a miraculous change in these elements, as they affirm, the Scripture would not have concealed it, but would have expressed it. Since however there is no mention of this change in the Scriptures, therefore there is no such change in this action. Moreover, if there were such a change, as they speak of, it would be either before or after the words of consecration are spoken; if the change is before the words of consecration are spoken, the consecration is

---

[2] See footnote on p. 115.

superfluous, and their proposition is false; if the change is after the words are spoken, viz. 'For this is my Body', their proposition is also false, because the word 'bread' is spoken before the last syllable of these five words is pronounced. These and many more absurdities follow from this doctrine.

And yet they obstinately persevere and urge upon us the letter of the Scripture, affirming that the words of Christ are so plain that they admit no figurative meaning. They would have spoken more advisedly if they had sought counsel of Augustine, in discerning between figurative speech and proper speech. In the third book and sixteenth chapter of his *Christian Doctrine* he says: 'If the speech seems to command any wickedness or mischief, or to forbid any happiness or welfare, it is not proper, but figurative speech.' And then he adds, as the example, a citation from John 6:53: 'Except ye eat the flesh of the Son of Man, and drink his blood, ye have no life in you.' To this Augustine adds: 'This speech appears to command a mischief, therefore it is figurative speech, through which we are commanded to have fellowship with the sufferings of Christ Jesus, and with gladness to keep in perpetual memory that the flesh of the Lord was crucified and wounded for us.' 'For otherwise', as the same author mentions, in his second book *Against the Adversaries of the Law and Prophets*, 'it would be more horrible really to eat the Flesh of Christ Jesus than to murder Him, and more horrible to drink His Blood than to shed His Blood.' Nevertheless, those who teach transubstant-iation still keep to the same tune, and maintain that these words ought to be taken literally. Thus it appears that they will not acknowledge this to be sacramental speech, acting out of sheer malice, and simply in order to contradict and withstand the truth. For they are compelled, whether they will or not, in other sayings of this sort, to acknowledge a figure, as in Genesis 17:10, where circumcision is called 'The Covenant'; in Exodus 12:11, where the Lamb is called 'the Passover'; in Matthew 26:28, where the Cup is called 'His Blood'; in Luke 22:20, where the Cup is called 'the New Testament'; and in 1 Corinthians 10:4, where the Rock is called 'Christ'. In all these passages the speech is sacramental, and receives a corresponding kind of interpretation; yet they maliciously insist on denying us in these five words (*hoc est enim corpus meum*) what they are compelled to grant in the rest, especially in the passage where Paul calls the Rock 'Christ.'

God does not will what is contrary to His nature

Now when they are driven out of this fortress, they fly as unhappily to a second, namely, that God by His omnipotence can make the Body of Christ be both in heaven and in the bread at the same time, therefore, they say, it is so. If I denied their conclusion, they would have much trouble in proving it; but the question at issue here is not whether God can do a thing or not, but whether God will do it or not, or whether He may will it or not. And we say reverently that His Majesty may not will it; even if it is true that He may do many things which He does not will, yet it is as true that there are many things which He may not will. These things are of two kinds: *First*, He may not will those things which are contrary to His nature, such as to be changeable, to decay, and so on; for if He might will these things, they would not be arguments for any might or power, but rather certain arguments for His impotence and infirmity. And therefore even if He may not will these

129

things, He does not cease to be omnipotent, but rather is His constant and invincible power all the more known.

God does not contradict what he has already decreed

Secondly, God may not will some things, because He has already decreed the contrary. This is the kind of thing we are now discussing; for since God has decreed that every human body should consist of organic parts, and therefore should be comprehended and circumscribed, within its own individual and proper place, and also since He has appointed Christ Jesus to have such a body, not just for a time, but eternally, therefore, I say, God may not now will the contrary, either to abolish this body, which He has appointed to be eternal, or yet to make it at one and the same time, a body and not a body, with quantity and without quantity, finite and infinite, with location and without location. He may no more will these things which are plain contradictions in themselves, than He can will a lie. Thus it may be seen of all men that we preserve the omnipotence of God and with reverence in our hearts acknowledge Him alone to be omnipotent; and we desire all men to esteem as calumniators those who abuse the ears of the simple by persuading them of the contrary to what we teach.

They are not content with this, for they say that the Lord may will a contradiction and make both parts to be true at one and the same time. To prove this they want to bring in the miracles which God works, as if they would say: every miracle involves a contradiction. For example, God made a virgin to bear a son. They think this work involves a contradiction; to bear a son is one part of the contradiction, and to be a virgin is the other part. This work is a miracle, but it implies no contradiction. It is indeed a miracle that a virgin should bear a son contrary to the course of nature, but to be a virgin and yet to have a child are not contradictory, if she has conceived and brought forth miraculously, as did the Blessed Virgin; but to be a virgin and not a virgin at the same time—this is a contradiction. So for Christ's Body to be visible and invisible, local and not local, at one and the same time, is, in every respect, the same contradiction, and therefore it cannot be true.

In another example, they speak of Christ's entering in when the doors were closed and shut, but what contradiction does there appear there? Can they prove that He entered through the doors, and if He did, then there was an alteration of qualities, and that by a miracle, either in Christ's body, or in the doors? But there is no contradiction in nature unless you do not know what a contradiction is. The third and last example they give is of the fire in Nebuchudnezzar's furnace, which consumed the servants but did not hurt those who were in the midst of the fire. This does not appear to have any more weight than the example we have already answered. They apparently imagine that in every miracle, contradiction is implied, which is absurd. If they can prove that this fire was both hot and cold, then they speak to some purpose, but that it burns up some and does not hurt others, is no contradiction, because its force was miraculously repressed. Thus the second argument holds fast: God may not will that which implies a contradiction. But the real presence of the Body of Christ in the Sacrament does imply a contradiction, for it makes the Body of Christ visible and invisible, compassed and not compassed, at one and the same time. Therefore God may not will such a thing.

When they are driven out of this, they make their last refuge an obstinate defense of their own opinion, for they say that Christ's Body is exempted from physical rules, for theology is not subject to physical rules. It is a very poor conclusion to say that we subject theology to physics because we defend the natural properties of the true and natural Body of Christ Jesus, first according to theology which is the law of God, and then according to physics, which is the law of nature. Granted that theology is not subject to physics, what of that? Therefore, Christ's body is exempted from physical rules. How does that follow, I pray? By what law may you exempt or can you exempt the Body of Christ? You cannot do it by the law of nature, for He was made of the seed of David, and took on Him true Flesh from the womb of the Virgin. Far less can you exempt the Body of Christ by the law of God, which is theology, for you know that Christ was appointed from all eternity to take on Himself our nature, and become true man. Indeed it is true that the law of God cannot be subject to the law of nature, for the law of nature flows out of the law of God, as out of its own spring. But it is as true that if you exempt Christ's Body from the law of nature, you will also exempt it from the law of God; for I affirm that the Scriptures so agree with the law of nature, that if you deny the one, you will deny the other, and if you admit the one, you will also admit the other. Therefore if you look well about you, you shall find the beam in your own eye, for you pervert both the law of God, and the law of nature, by a newly invented physics of your own. For he who attributes to one and the self-same body natural and unnatural properties, which directly fight against each other, perverts both true theology and physics. But to one and the self-same body of Christ Jesus, you attribute natural and unnatural properties; therefore it is you who pervert both the use of true theology and the order set down and established in nature. Would you know the reason for my proposition? I say that in theology as well as in physics, one of two contradictory statements must necessarily be false. But now to make an end with you, once for all, we shall answer your last subterfuge.

Christ's glorified Body is not against nature

They reason thus: a glorified being is not subject to natural laws, but Christ's Body is glorified, therefore it is not subject to natural laws. First of all, before we answer directly, we must consider what the glorification of the body consists of, and then the answer will be easy. In 1 Corinthians 15:42, the apostle Paul has this to say: 'So also is the resurrection of the dead: the body is sown in corruption, and is raised in incorruption. It is sown in dishonour, and is raised in glory. It is sown in weakness, and is raised in power.' And, a little later, 'This corruptible must put on incorruption, and this mortal must put on immortality.' By this clear antithesis, Paul plainly describes the glorification of the body, for he opposes these two, the unglorified body, and the glorified body. To the unglorified body he ascribes corruption, ignominy, infirmity, carnality and mortality; to the glorified body he attributes incorruption, glory, power, spirituality and immortality. From this opposition we may easily gather what resurrection and glorification bring to the body, briefly: by them we see that the body is only deprived of corruption, shame, infirmity, naturality and mortality; and, in a word, it only loses all the infirmities of our nature that it may be clothed with the more glorious apparel with incorruption, power, glory, spirituality and immortality. We see then that this glorification does indeed bring a change. But I believe no man would be so mad as to think this change is made in the substance, for if it were, the old substance should decay, and a new one arise. But we hear of no such thing in this description. And as little is the change made in the quantity, for we hear no word either of augmentation or diminution of any substance, which ought to be the case if there were a change in the quantity. So far as we can perceive, this mutation consists in the quality by which the body casts off the old coat of infirmity and is clothed with the coat of glory; for Christ, after He rose, both went and came, was seen and touched.

From the things already deduced, it clearly follows that since the glory of the Body of Christ has wrought no change in His nature and substance, nor consequently in His natural dimensions, nor yet in any other essential property, therefore the glorification of His body does not exempt it from the laws of physics. So long as the nature of the true body remains, there are no supernatural gifts whereby it may be glorified—no matter how exalted they may be, as far as may be learned from the divine Scripture—that may hurt either its nature, or its natural property. For there is no gift nor quality that may hurt nature except the gift that is against nature. But the supernatural gift is neither unnatural nor against nature; therefore it cannot hurt or impair nature. And my reason is this: these gifts that decorate and beautify nature cannot hurt or impair nature; but all supernatural gifts decorate and beautify nature; therefore they cannot take away either nature or natural property.

They do not leave it there, but from this same doctrine of Paul concerning the glorification of the body, they derive another objection which they urge against us.

Paul grants that a glorified body is a spiritual body; but a spiritual body is an invisible body; therefore a glorified body is invisible, and consequently the Body of Christ is invisible. Even if this is not a formal argument, nevertheless, to be quite brief, I deny their assumption; for even if there were no more to it than the word 'body', that word would be an argument that the spiritual body is not invisible.

Let us open up the matter more clearly, according to the mind of Paul in this passage, 1 Corinthians 15. In the 44th verse of this chapter, he shows the change that will take place in the qualities of the body by the resurrection, for he says that from being a natural body, it will become a spiritual body. Then in the very next verse he expounds these two qualities, saying: 'that is called a natural body which is maintained and quickened by a living soul only, such as Adam's was. And again, that is said to be a spiritual body which together with the soul is quickened by a far more excellent virtue, namely by the Spirit of God, sent to us from Christ the second Adam.' Then in line with this I answer with Augustine in *Ad Constantium*: 'As the natural body is not a soul, but a body, even so the spiritual body is not said to be a soul, but a body, and consequently it is invisible.'

In taking up this point, I shall give them only one knot to loosen, and so make an end of it. I reason thus: if Christ's Body is naturally and really in the Supper, because it is glorified, it follows that when it was not glorified it could not be really present; but it was not glorified when this Supper was first instituted, and therefore it was not really present in the bread at Christ's first Supper. If His Body was not actually present in the bread at the first Supper, it cannot be naturally present now, for whatever they use now in the administration of their Supper, or of their Mass (call it what they will), according to their own confession, they use it according to the ordinance, form and manner that Christ Himself used in His first Supper. For they say plainly in their disputation at Poissy (in 1561) and in all the rest of their works, that Christ Jesus first of all observed that form which they use in their Mass, and left it to His apostles and to their successors that they should do the same. Thus by their own words they have entangled themselves in their own net, and crucified their Mass. What can they answer to this? They will not stand dumb, I am sure, for they must say something to maintain their religion, since if this argument is valid, they are finished with it.

The Papists answer that even if the Body of Christ which was locally present with the rest of His disciples was not glorified, nevertheless the Body which He exhibited in the bread was glorified, they might as well have held their peace and said nothing. For consider the words of the text as they are written in Luke 22:17: 'And He took bread, and when he had given thanks, he brake it, and gave to them, saying, "This is my body which is given for you"'; and the words of St. Paul in 1 Corinthians 11:24: 'Take, eat, this is my body which is broken for you.' This 'which' refers to the Body exhibited in the bread, for according to their own confession, these words are pronounced upon the bread, and directed to it. But that same body was given and broken for us, that is to say, crucified and humiliated with anguish and sorrow. Then I reason thus: to be crucified and broken with anguish and sorrow cannot in any way be consistent with a glorified body, but the Body that Christ exhibited in the bread is said by the evangelists to be crucified and broken for us, therefore that body was not glorified.

Now, last of all, they still refuse to be satisfied, and say Christ can make the bread His Body, and therefore His Body is really present. We grant that Christ can make the bread His Body, for Christ being God can do whatever He will; only let them show that Christ will make the real bread His real Flesh, and then this controversy is brought to an end. Christ does indeed make the bread His Body, not really, but sacramentally, for Christ does not have a Body made of bread. His Body was made once for all of the pure substance of His blessed mother. He does not have any other Body than this, or one made more often than once. Wherefore all doctrine that teaches that Christ's Body is made of bread is impious and heretical. The Papists' doctrine of a real presence teaches that Christ's Body in the Sacrament is made of bread, by changing the bread into His Body through the power of concentration, therefore we may boldly and truly conclude that their doctrine of a real presence is both wicked and heretical. Now in concluding this section, I beseech them, since reason fails them, not to fight against God in order to maintain a lie, however old it may be (for the devil is old enough, and yet he could never change his nature!) but let them rather glorify God, in confessing these words to be sacramental.

The five words must be spiritually understood

What then is the reason why the Papists draw down the substance of the Body of Christ and the Blood of Christ, and make the very substance to be corporally, really, and substantially in the Sacrament? The reason is this: They cannot see by their natural judgement, nor understand by their natural intelligence, this truth, how Christ's Flesh and Blood can be present in the Sacrament without being present in their corporal hands and in their corporal mouths and stomachs. If they had any light to show them that Christ may be present in the Supper and not in the hand, the mouth or the stomach, they would never have thought of such an absurd presence as they reckon to be there. But being destitute of spiritual light, they follow their natural reason, and make it out to be a natural and carnal presence. Thus we have this lesson to learn here: no man who has not the Spirit of God can understand these five words, 'For this is my body'. Such a man will without doubt do as the Papists do, that is, he will understand it carnally. Thus since they mistake its true meaning, it is not surprising that they and we differ in this matter.

If you ask the Papist first if the true Body of Christ is there, or if the true Flesh and Blood of Christ are there, he will say, they are. If you ask, 'In what?' he will say, 'In and under the accidents of the bread and wine, under the colour and roundness of the bread'. If you ask him again, 'By what instrument are they received?' he will tell you, 'By the mouth and stomach of the body'. Such is their gross understanding of the Body and Blood of Christ. If you ask about the ubiquity, if the true Body of Christ is present, he will say it is. If you ask, is it in, with or under the bread, he will answer, it is in the bread as its content, that is, the bread contains it. If you ask him to what instrument is it offered, he will answer, the Body and the Blood of Christ are offered to the mouth of our body.

Christ's Body is present by the Holy Spirit through faith

If you ask of us, on the other hand, how the true Body and Blood of Christ Jesus are present, we will say that they are spiritually present, really present, that is, present in the Supper, and not in the bread. We will not say that His true Flesh is present in our hands, or in the mouth of our body, but that it is spiritually present, that is, present to our spirits, and our believing soul—yes, even as present inwardly in our souls, as the bread and wine are present to the body outwardly. If you ask them whether the Body and Blood of Christ Jesus are present in the Supper, we answer in a word, 'They are present in the Supper, but not in the bread and wine, nor in the accidents or substance of bread and wine'. We hold that Christ is present in the Supper because He is present to our soul, to our spirit and faith; also we hold that He is present in the Supper because we have Him in His promise 'This is my body'. This promise is present in my faith, and the nature of faith is to make things that are absent in themselves, present nevertheless. And therefore since He is both present by faith in His promise and present by the power of His Holy Spirit, who can deny that He is present in the Supper?

Nevertheless it should be explained what we mean by the word 'present'—how a thing is said to be present and absent. In knowing this we shall find it all quite easy. Things are said to be present as they are perceived by any outward or inward sense, and as they are perceived by any of the senses; the more they are perceived, the more present they are, and by whatever sense anything is perceived, to that sense it is present. If therefore it is outwardly perceived by an outward presence, the thing is outwardly present; for example, if it is perceived by the outward sight of the eye, by the outward hearing of

139

the ear, by the outward feeling of the hands, or taste of the mouth, it is outwardly present; if however anything is perceived by the inward eye, by the inward taste and feeling of the soul, it cannot be outwardly present, but must be spiritually and inwardly present to the soul; therefore everything is present as it is perceived, so that if you do not perceive a thing outwardly, it is outwardly absent, and if you do not perceive a thing inwardly, it is inwardly absent. It is not distance of place that makes a thing absent, or nearness of place that makes a thing present, but it is only the perception of anything by any of your senses that makes a thing present, and it is the absence of perception that makes a thing absent. Even if the thing itself were never so far distant, if you perceive it by your outward sense, it is present to you. For example, my body and the sun are as far distant in place as the heaven is from the earth, and yet this distance does not keep the sun's presence away from me. Why? Because I perceive the sun by my eye and my other senses, I feel it and perceive it by its heat, by its light, and by its brightness. Therefore if a thing is ever so far distant, if we have senses to perceive it, it is present to us. The distance of place, then, does not make a thing absent from you, if you have senses to perceive it. Likewise the nearness of a place does not make a thing present, even if it is ever so near, if you have no senses to perceive it. For example, if the sun shines upon your eyes, if you are blind, it is not present to you, because you cannot perceive it. A sweet tune will never be present to a deaf ear, even though it is sung in the ear of that man, because he has not a sense to perceive it; and a well-told tale will never be present to a fool, because he cannot understand it, and has no judgement to perceive it. Thus it is not nearness or distance of place that makes anything present or absent, but only the perceiving or not perceiving of it.

Now, you ask, how is the Body of Christ present? In a word, as you have heard, from time to time, He is present not to the outward senses, but to the inward senses, which is faith wrought in the soul. For this action of the Sacrament and of the Supper is partly corporal, and partly spiritual. I call this action partly corporal, not only because the objects, that is, the bread and wine, are corporal, but also because my mouth, to which these things are offered, the instrument by which and the manner in which these things are received, are all corporal and natural. I call the same action again partly spiritual, not only because of Christ Jesus, who is the heavenly and spiritual thing in the Sacrament, but also because of my soul, to which Christ is offered and given, because of the instrument by which, and the manner in which He is received, are all spiritual; for I do not get Christ corporally, but spiritually. So in these respects I call this action partly corporal, and partly spiritual.

Now, *first* do not confound these two kinds of action, the corporal and natural signs, with the spiritual thing signified by them. *Again*, do not confound the mouth of the body with the mouth of the soul. *Thirdly*, do not confound the outward manner of receiving by the hand of the body, with the spiritual manner of receiving by the hand of the soul. In this way it will be seen very clearly that each thing is present to its own instrument; that is, the Body of Christ, which is the spiritual thing signified, is present to the spiritual mouth and hand, and the bread and the wine, which are the corporal signs, are present to the corporal mouth and hand. Then, how is any object present? A corporal object is corporally present, and an inward object is inwardly present. What is the nature of the thing signified? It is of a heavenly nature. Then you ask, how is He present? He is present in a spiritual and heavenly way to your soul, and the mouth of your soul, which is faith. It would be a preposterous thing to make the thing signified present to your stomach, or to your mouth, or to the eye of your body, for if it were, it would not be spiritually present, because everything is present in accordance with its own nature. If it is a bodily thing, it is present in a bodily way, and if it is a heavenly thing, it is present in a spiritual way. Therefore I do not think anyone can doubt how the Body of Christ is present. He is not carnally present, but spiritually present to my soul, and to faith in my soul. So much concerning the manner of His presence.

Communicants are addressed, not the elements

Now we come to the last point in our discussion. We have to consider to whom the words ought to be directed and pronounced, for we and the Papists differ on this point. We say that the words ought to be directed and pronounced to the people, to the faithful communicants; they, on the contrary, say that the words ought not to be directed or be pronounced to the people, but to the elements, and that they ought not to be clearly pronounced, but whispered over the elements, so that if they are spoken to the people, or spoken plainly, their charm is of no avail. Now I say that as this action is perverted by them in all its other parts, so it is perverted at this point also, when they speak to the dumb elements what they ought to speak to the people of God. I shall prove this clearly by three arguments taken out of the Scriptures, that the words ought not to be spoken to the bread, but to the people of God.

Firstly, the promises of mercy and grace ought to be directed and pronounced to those in whom the Lord performs them, and makes them effectual. The promises of mercy and grace, however, are performed and made effectual not in bread and wine, but in faithful men and women. Therefore these promises should be directed to faithful men and women. Now here is the promise of mercy and grace: 'This is my body, which is broken for you.' This promise is not made to any thing, but to faithful men and women, and so it ought to be directed to them only.

Secondly, we have to consider the fact that this Sacrament seals up a Covenant of grace and mercy. Now, with whom does God make His Covenant of mercy and grace? Will He make a covenant with a piece of bread, or with any dumb element? There is no man who will enter into a covenant with his servant, not to mention entering into a covenant with a dumb element. Therefore, because the Sacrament seals up a covenant, this covenant must of necessity be made with a faithful soul, and not with the dumb element, and therefore these words cannot be directed to the elements.

Thirdly, consider the end for which this Sacrament was appointed. Is it not to lead us to Christ, is it not to nourish our faith in Christ, is it not to nourish us in a constant persuasion of the Lord's mercy in Christ? Was the Sacrament appointed to make the elements gods? No, for if you mark God's purpose in this institution, you will find that Christ has not established it to ennoble the elements, to favour and honour the elements, which were bread and wine yesterday, making them into gods today. We, on the contrary, say plainly that the institution of Christ is not concerned with the elements in altering their nature, indeed it is appointed to alter us, to change us, and to make us more and more spiritual, and to sanctify the elements to our use. But the special end is this: to make us holy, and more and more to grow up in a sure faith in Christ, and not to alter the elements or to make them gods. Therefore, by all these three arguments it is evident that the words ought not to be directed to the elements, but to the people and faithful communicants.

Now, in conclusion, there is one thing without which we cannot gain any benefit, no matter how long we discourse upon the proper understanding of the Sacrament. As you see, all that is spoken concerning the Sacrament is grounded and depends upon *faith*. If a man has faith, even if it is ever so little, he gets some hold on Christ, and some insight in the understanding of this Sacrament; but if he is without faith, even if a man takes trouble to make the Sacraments ever so clear, it is not possible for him to get any hold of Christ or any insight in Him. Without faith we cannot be Christians, nor can we see God or feel God in Christ without faith. Faith is the only thing that translates our souls out of the death and damnation in which we were conceived and born, and plants us into life. Thus all the study and endeavour of a Christian should be directed to this, to ask that the Lord in His mercy may enlighten his mind with the eye of faith, and kindle in his heart a love of faith, and work in his heart a thirst and desire for the object of faith, and more and more to thirst and hunger for the food of faith, that nourishes us to life eternal.

144

Without this faith (no matter how much the natural man may flatter himself in his natural understanding) there is certainly no blessedness, but all his life is nothing but terrible misery. Whatever it is that flatters and pleases you now, whether it be a thought or motion of the mind, or an action of the body, without faith the very same motion, cogitation and action will torment you hereafter. Thus without faith it is not possible to please God, and whatever does not please God, is done to torment you. Therefore ask mercy for any motion, cogitation or action in which you have offended God, or else God will offend and punish you in those very things. There is no way to avoid offending God except by true faith; therefore the Christian should strive to grow in faith.

Now it is through hearing the Word that you get faith, and by receiving the Sacrament that you get the increase of faith; and when you have faith, the receiving of the Sacrament will be fruitful, but without faith you eat your own condemnation. Therefore the whole aim of a Christian is to get faith, and this faith cannot be obtained in idleness, but by earnest prayer. Therefore let every one of us fall down and earnestly pray for this faith, and its increase, in which we may be worthy receivers of this Sacrament, through the righteous merits of Christ Jesus, to whom with the Father and the Holy Spirit be all honour, praise and glory, now and for ever. Amen.

4

THE PREPARATION FOR
THE LORD'S SUPPER 1

But let a man examine himself and so let him eat of that bread, and drink of that cup.

THE doctrine of our trial and due examination, well beloved in Christ Jesus, ought to come before the doctrine and receiving of the Sacrament. No man can hear the Word of God fruitfully without in some measure preparing his soul, and preparing the ear of his heart to hear, but preparation is always just as necessary for the receiving of the visible Sacrament as for the hearing of the simple Word. Therefore the doctrine of preparation and due examination should be given its proper place, and is very necessary for every one of you.

In the words that we have read, the Apostle offers his counsel and gives his advice, and not only his advice, but his admonition and command, that we should not come to the Table of the Lord, or come to the hearing of the Word rashly, but that every one of us should come to this holy action with reverence, that we should prepare and sanctify ourselves in some measure. Since we go to the Table of the King of heaven, it becomes us to put on our best apparel. In a word, he sets forth the whole doctrine and matter of such preparation when he says:

'Let every man and every woman try and examine themselves'.

It is as if he would say: 'Let every one of you try and examine your soul, that is, try the state of your own heart, and the condition of your own conscience. See what is the state of your heart with God, and what is the state of your conscience with your neighbour.' He does not ask your neighbour to try you; he does not ask your companion to try your heart; but he bids you personally to try your own conscience, and try your own heart, for no one can be certain of the state of your heart, or of the condition of your conscience, but you yourself. Now, he does not exclude others from proving you, for it is the part of the pastor to try you, but no others can try you as strictly as you yourself can, for no man can know as much of you as you know of yourself. No one else can be certain of the state of your heart and the condition of your conscience, but you yourself may be certain of it. As for others, they may judge your heart and conscience according to your works and fruits, and unless your works and fruits are very wicked, and altogether vicious, we are bound in conscience to judge charitably of your heart and conscience. Thus no one is so fit to try the spirit of a man, to try the heart or conscience of a man as the man himself.

If this trial is to be carried through well, three things have to be considered:—*First*, you have to understand what it is that you are to try; what you call a conscience, which the Apostle commands you to try. *Secondly*, you have to weigh and consider the reasons and grounds why you should try your conscience. *Thirdly*, you have to see what the chief points are in which you should try and examine your conscience.

1. The necessity of understanding our consciences

First, to begin with what is known to each of you, for there is none of you who lacks a conscience, it is necessary to understand what a conscience is. Therefore, as far as God gives me grace, I will explain it to you. I call a conscience a certain feeling in the heart, resembling the judgement of the living God, following upon a deed done by us, flowing from a knowledge in the mind, and accompanied by a certain motion of the heart, fear or joy, trembling or rejoicing.

[1] Now let us examine the different parts of this definition. I call it first of all *a certain feeling in the heart*, for the Lord has left such a stamp in the heart of every man that he does not do anything so secretly or quietly without making his own heart strike him and smite him. God makes him feel in his own heart whether he has done well or ill. Why has the Lord placed this feeling in the heart? Because the eyes of God do not look so much upon the outward countenance and external behaviour, as upon the inward heart. For He says to Samuel in his first Book (16:7), 'The Lord beholds the heart.' Likewise in 1 Chronicles 28:9, He says to Solomon, 'The Lord searcheth all hearts, and understandeth all the imaginations of the thoughts.' Also Jeremiah 11:20 says, 'The Lord tries the reins and the heart.' And the Apostle in 1 Corinthians 4:5 says: 'The Lord will bring to light the hidden things of darkness, and make manifest the counsels of the hearts.' Therefore, because the Lord is concerned chiefly with

148

the heart, it is in the heart that He places this feeling, which is the chief part of conscience.

[2] Then I say that this feeling *resembles the judgement of God*, for this feeling was left and placed in our soul in order that we might have a domestic and familiar judgement within ourselves, to subscribe to and resemble the secret and invisible judgement of the high God—a particular judgement to go before that general judgement in that great day when every man shall be justified or damned, according to the particular judgement that is within his own conscience. In the meantime, this conscience is left in us as the means whereby the living God relates His acts in the Last Judgement to the whole process of our life on earth. For the books of our own conscience in that Last Day will be opened, and every man shall receive according to the report of the decree within his own conscience. Therefore, I say, our conscience resembles the judgement of God.

[3] The third thing that I say is that it *follows upon a deed done by us*. Our conscience does not smite us before the deed is done, our heart does not strike us before the evil deed is committed. No, the stroke of the conscience and the feeling of the heart do not precede, but follow immediately upon the deed. Thus the deed is no sooner done, than your conscience applies it to yourself, and gives out the sentence against you. Therefore, I say, it is a feeling following upon a deed done by us.

[4] The fourth thing that I say is that it is a feeling *flowing from a knowledge in the mind*, for unless the conscience is informed and the heart knows that the

thing which is done is evil, neither the heart nor the conscience can ever count it to be evil. Knowledge must go before the stroke of the conscience. Your heart can never feel that to be evil which your mind does not know to be evil. Therefore knowledge must ever go before feeling, and the testimony and stroke of your conscience will be in accordance with the measure of your knowledge. For a slight knowledge, a doubting and uncertain knowledge, makes the stroke of the conscience light and small, as on the other hand, a holy and solid knowledge drawn from the Word of God, makes the stroke of the conscience heavy. Thus the conscience must answer to knowledge. If we have no other knowledge but the knowledge which we have by nature, and by the spark of light still left in nature, our conscience will answer no further than to that knowledge. But if beside the light of nature we have a knowledge of God and His Word, and a knowledge of God by His Holy Spirit working in our hearts, then our conscience will go further, excusing or accusing us, according to the light that is in the Word. Thus the conscience is not acquired, or attained at the time we are enlightened by the working of the Holy Spirit and hearing of the Word of God; but our conscience is born with us, is natural to us, and is left in the soul of every man and woman. As there are some sparks of light left in nature, so there is a conscience left in it also. And if there were no more than that, that very light left in your nature would be enough to condemn you. The conscience is not acquired, therefore, nor does it begin with the hearing of the Word, or at the time when we begin to reform ourselves by the assistance and renewing of the Holy Spirit. Every man by nature has a conscience, and the Lord has left it in our nature. And even if this natural conscience is not reformed according to the Word of God, it will be enough to condemn you eternally. Therefore, I speak of the feeling in the heart as *flowing from a knowledge of the mind.*

[5] Last of all I say that it is *accompanied with a certain motion of the heart*; and we express this motion in fear or joy, trembling or rejoicing. It will be in very great fear, if the deed is exceedingly heinous, and the stroke of the conscience is very heavy—then the conscience is never at rest, for guilt must always involve dread. But if the deed is honest, godly and commendable, it makes the heart glad, and even to break forth in joy. Thus, to be brief, in every conscience there must be two things: there must be a knowledge, and there must be a feeling whereby, according to your knowledge, you apply to your own heart the deed you have done. Thus, as the very word itself indicates, conscience consists of two parts: of knowledge, according to which it is called *science,* and of feeling, according to which the *con* is added—therefore *conscience.* The word conscience signifies, therefore, knowledge with application.

This conscience the Lord has appointed to serve in the soul of man for many uses, namely, to act as a keeper, a companion, a careful attendant on every action you do. Therefore, no action can be accomplished so secretly, so quietly, so surreptitiously, but that, whether you will or not, your conscience will bear testimony to it. Your conscience will be a faithful observer of it, and one day, a faithful recorder of that same action. And so (1) the Lord has appointed your conscience to this office, that it may attend and wait upon you, in all your actions; nothing can escape it. (2) Likewise, the Lord has appointed your conscience, and placed it in your soul, to be your accuser, so that when you do any evil deed, you have a private accuser within your own soul, to find fault with it. And (3) He has also placed it within your soul to be a true and steadfast witness against you. Yes, the testimony of the conscience not only resembles a testimony or a witness, but the conscience is as good as ten thousand witnesses. (4) The conscience is also left in your soul to act the part of a judge against you, to declare the sentence against you, to condemn you. And so it does, for our particular judgement must precede the general and universal judgement of the Lord at that great Day. And what more? (5) He has left your conscience within you to put your own sentence into execution against yourself. This is terrible. He has left it within you to be a torment and a scourge to yourself, and so to put your own sentence into execution.

Is not this something more than wonderful, that one and the self-same conscience should serve so many ends in a soul, as to be a continual observer and marker of your actions, an accuser, ten thousand witnesses, a judge, an executioner and tormentor, to execute your own sentence against yourself? Thus the Lord never needs to seek a member of court outside of your own soul in order to conduct a lawful process against you, for you have all these within yourself. Take note of this, for there is not a word of this that shall fall to the ground, but you will find it either to your weal, or to your everlasting woe. This secret and particular judgement that everyone of you carries about with you, remains so surely and firmly embedded within you, that do what you can to blot it out, you will never get it eradicated from your soul. If you were to become as malicious and as wicked as ever any incarnate devil upon the earth, you would never get this conscience altogether eradicated from your soul; but, whether you will or not, there would always remain sufficient of it to make you inexcusable in the great Day of the general Judgement.

I grant that you may blot out all knowledge from your mind, and make yourself as blind as a mole; I grant also that you may harden your heart so as to blot out all feeling from it, so that your conscience will not accuse you, or find fault with you, and you will even have a delight in doing evil without any remorse, but I deny that any degree of wickedness on the earth will bring you to the point where you may do evil without fear. The more you do evil, the longer you continue in evil-doing, the greater will be your fear. Yes, in spite of the devil, and in spite of all the malice of the heart of man, that fear will remain. And even if they should both conspire together, it would not be in their power to banish that fear, for the gnawing of the conscience will ever remain to testify to you that there is a Day of Judgement.

I grant also that conditions will change from time to time, that fear will not always remain, but will sometimes give way to security. Neither will that security always remain, but will give way again to fear, so that it will not be possible to get this fear wholly eradicated. The greater the security is, the greater will your fear be when you are awakened.

I grant, again, that this fear will be blind, for from the time a man by evil-doing has banished knowledge from his mind, and feeling from his heart, what can there remain, but a blind fear? When men have put out all light and left nothing in their nature but darkness, there can remain nothing but a blind fear. So I grant that fear is blind, for neither do they know where fear comes from, what progress it makes, and where it leads to, nor do they know where and when it will end. Therefore those who are in this way misguided in their souls are of all men on earth the most miserable. As long as you keep in your mind a spark of this knowledge and spiritual light, by which you may see the face of God in Christ, by which you may see an escape in the death and passion of Christ, and by which you may see God's compassionate mercy offered in the Blood of Christ, if you have any spark of this light, even if it be ever so little, to direct you, and even if this knowledge were very severely damaged, yet there is mercy enough for you in Christ. But if you close up all the windows of your soul and your heart, and fill them with palpable darkness, so that you neither know where the terror comes from, nor see any way of escaping it, that is the misery of all miseries.

We have much to lament; we have the state of this country to lament, for they are not present to whom this preaching specially applies. Even so, there is not one of you who should not now take heed to your conscience, while leisure is given to you, in order that you may not banish altogether this light which is still offered to you, some sparks of which still remain. I see most of our great men in this country running headlong to extinguish the spark of light that is in them, and they will not rest until it is utterly extinguished. And when they have done so, what can follow, alas, but a blind and terrible fear in their conscience which they can never have eradicated—a fear without a way of escape, a fear that grows and does not decay, a fear that will devour them wholly at the last. Therefore let everyone of you take heed to this light that is within you, take heed that the foul affections of your heart do not draw your bodies after them; see at least that these affections do not banish this light. And so long as the Lord offers you this light in time, pray that in His mercy He may give you the grace to embrace it, to enter a new course, and to amend your lives while you still have time.

The body will leave the soul, and the soul will leave the body, but the conscience will never leave the soul. But wherever the soul goes, to the same place will the conscience repair, and in whatever state your conscience is, when you die, in the same state it will meet you on that great Day. Therefore if your conscience is a torment to you at the time of your death, if you do not get it pacified then, it will be your executioner at the final Judgement.

Therefore this matter must be well considered, and every one of you should endeavour to have a good conscience, that when the soul is severed from the body, leaving your conscience at rest and peace with God, it may be restored to you, and meet you again with as great peace and quietness. So much, then, for the conscience, and what it is. I pray that the Living God may so sanctify your memories that you may keep these things, and that every one of them may remain with you in such a way that to the end of your life you may remember them.

2. Why should each of us examine ourselves?

The second thing we have to speak of is this: we must try to consider why we should examine our conscience. What are the reasons that should move men or women to try their own consciences and souls? I shall answer briefly.

[1] It becomes every one of you to try your conscience because the Lord makes His residence in it, and in no other part of the soul. He has appointed His dwelling to be in the heart of man, in his will and conscience, and therefore it becomes you to make His dwelling-place clean, and to take heed to your heart.

[2] Even if the Lord of heaven were not to make His residence there, nevertheless the eye of God is all-seeing, able to pierce through the thickness of man's flesh, however dark and gross it may be, and to pierce right through into the secret corners of your conscience. To the all-seeing eye of God, the most secret corner of your conscience is as open, clear and manifest as any outward or bodily thing on earth can be to the outward eye of the body. Therefore because His eye is so piercing and because He casts His eye only upon our heart, it becomes us to try our hearts.

[3] He is the Lord of the conscience. No earthly monarch has any sovereignty or lordship over the conscience. Only the God of heaven, only Christ Jesus, King of heaven and earth, is Lord of the conscience. He only has power to save and loose. Therefore when you prepare to come to the Lord's Table, is it not fitting that you should look at your conscience, to test and examine its state?

[4] One of the chief reasons why it becomes you to try and examine your conscience is because the health and welfare of your soul depends upon it. If your conscience within your soul is well, if it is at peace and rest, your soul is well. If your conscience is in a good state, your soul must be in a good state. If your conscience is in good health, your soul must necessarily be in good health, for the good health and weal of your soul depends upon a good conscience. Therefore it becomes every one of you to try your conscience well. No law was ever set down or devised that made it unlawful for us to take care of ourselves. It is lawful for us to seek the things that procure, preserve and maintain our health. Now, since the health of your soul consists in the health of your conscience, and in preserving it, therefore in accordance with all law, you ought to attend to your conscience. If you keep your conscience well, your soul is in health, and if your soul is in health, no matter what troubles may come upon your body, you will endure them all. But if your soul is diseased, and if that pining sickness brought on by an evil conscience lays hold upon your soul, you will not be able to endure the smallest trouble that can come upon your body; whereas if the conscience is at rest and in good health, no trouble can come upon your body but the strength of a good conscience will be more than a match for it. Have you not reason, therefore, and more than reason, to take heed to your conscience, to examine and to try its state and disposition?

Now, because it is a tasteless jest to tell you that health is necessary, and not to show you how that health may be acquired, preserved, and maintained, therefore to keep your conscience in quietness and in good health,

I shall give you these few lessons. (1) First of all, take care to keep a steadfast persuasion of the mercy of God in Christ Jesus. When you lie down, and when you rise up, examine your relation with God, and see whether you may look for mercy at His hand or not. Are you persuaded of His mercy? Be assured, then, that your conscience is in a good condition, that you have health in your soul; for by the keeping of faith, the conscience is preserved, as the apostle says in 1 Timothy 1 :19. Keep this persuasion, preserve it whole and sound; do not hurt it; try not to let your soul into doubt; do not let anything hinder your persuasion, if you would keep your soul in health. If you doubt or in any way weaken your persuasion and assurance, then assuredly there will follow at the same time loss of health in your soul. It is inevitable, too, that your conscience will be hurt at the same time, and faith will not dwell except in a healthy conscience. Therefore whenever you do anything against your conscience, you immediately weaken your persuasion of the mercy of God, and you will continue to doubt His mercy and want health in your conscience until you fall down at the feet of Christ, obtain mercy for that evil deed, gain peace at His hand, and repair your persuasion. This then in the first lesson: in order to preserve your souls in health, be sure that you are persuaded of God's mercy.

(2) The second lesson is this: you must flee, eschew and forbear whatever may trouble the health of your soul, whatever may trouble the quietness and peace of your conscience. Cast it out, refuse to have anything to do with it. In general, that is the right thing to do, but let us see what it is that troubles the quiet state of conscience. Nothing in the world but sin, nothing on

earth but an evil nature. Therefore, if we are to keep our soul in health, we must necessarily avoid sin altogether, we must flee from it, and get rid of it. It is not possible both to keep a good conscience, and to serve the affections of your heart; and therefore if you are to keep peace and health in your soul, you must bid goodnight to your lusts and renounce the affections of your heart. You must not do as you were wont to do, in fulfilling your own affections and appetites. What are you to do, then, when your affections or lusts command you to do something? You must examine how far this is consistent with the good will of God, and how far the affection that commands you agrees with the law of God. If there is such an agreement between the affection that commands you and God's law and holy will, it is without doubt a sanctified affection, and you may fulfill it. But if afterwards you find your affection becoming exorbitant and inordinate, usurping God's will and opposing His law, beware of it. Beware lest you yield to it and fulfill it. Resist it. For if you were to fulfill the will of that affection, even for an hour, what pleasure could it bring with it? It may well bring with it a flattering pleasure to begin with, but it always finishes with a bitter remorse in the end.

Then to eschew this bitter remorse, should you not all try your affections? You must examine and try them by the measure of God's law. You must see how far they agree with His law, or how far they disagree with it; and in so far as they disagree with it, let every man deny himself, and renounce his affections. When you take this trial to yourself in this way, it sanctifies your affections, makes Christ lodge in your soul, gives your conscience rest. In this way the Holy Spirit makes both body and soul to be in good health, and rejoice. Therefore flee from sin. This is the second lesson.

(3) The third lesson is this: study to do well. If you want to keep health in your soul, study to do better and better continually, at least have a purpose in your heart to do better daily. That is the last lesson. Since even when we endeavour to do our best, we fall, since even the just man, the holiest man, falls as often as seven times a day, indeed, seventy times seven, what are you to do in these slips and falls? If you fall, and you cannot avoid it, do not lie still, do not sleep there where you have fallen. It would be a shame to sleep, therefore rise again. And how are you to rise? By lifting up your soul and running to the fountain of grace and mercy, by repairing to Christ Jesus, to obtain mercy for your soul, and to ask Him to send from Himself the needed peace to put your conscience to rest, and to restore your soul to health. Therefore do not lie where you fall, but rise at once and pray for mercy. In obtaining mercy you will recover from your fall; you will amend your life by repentance, and by repentance you will get peace. Then you will have a quiet conscience, and gain health for your soul.

Now keep this rule if you want to keep your soul in health: take care not to sleep in sin, as David did; do not lie still when you have fallen, and so fall from one sin into another, as from adultery to murder, and from murder to the next. As a rule, if a man sleeps in sin, and does not rise in time, one sin will lead to another, for no sin is ever alone. The greater and more heinous a sin is, the greater and the worse are the sins that follow upon it. Therefore when you fall, do not delay rising, but run to the fountain of mercy, and seek grace in time. Run to prayer, run to the Church of God, wherever it may be, whether in the field or in the town. Run to Christ Jesus, and ask for His mercy, that you may have peace in your consciences. And so by these means you will all preserve health in your souls. In this way you will learn the difference between this living Word of mercy and grace, which is to be heard in our religion, and the 'letter that killeth', which slays the soul of everyone that hears it—I mean that idolatrous doctrine of the Mass.

I refer to this because I see that our youth, for the most part, are given to it, and the Lord is beginning to remove His grace and mercy from this country, because of the contempt for this quickening Word which has so clearly sounded here, and which our noblemen (most of whom run headlong to the devil, as in a stupor) strive utterly to banish. Is not this a miserable thing, that none of you has eyes to consider and discern the time of peace, mercy and grace which is so abundantly offered? May the Lord in His mercy give you eyes in time.

So much, then, for the reasons why everyone of you should try and examine your own consciences, a trial that ought to take place not for a day or for a year, but one that ought to take place every day, and every year of your whole life. Because conscience must ever live with the living God, and must ever behold the face of the Son of God, it cannot be cleansed too thoroughly, or examined too carefully. The more anxious we are in searching the conscience, the better occupied we will be —I speak of our own conscience, not of our neighbour's.

3. The chief points in examining our consciences

Thirdly, I come to the point wherein everyone of you should try to examine yourself. Everyone of you ought to try and examine your conscience, *first*, as to whether you are at peace with God, who is the Lord of heaven, or not; *second*, as to whether you are in love and amity with your neighbour or not.

Do you want to know whether your conscience is *in harmony and peace with God*, or not? You can know it in this way: the God of heaven cannot have any fellowship or company with the soul that is always unclean, and altogether defiled. No, He cannot. Now, I do not mean to say that a soul can be fully sanctified and perfectly holy in this life; no, in this life there are astonishing iniquities, gross sins and great faults, with which even the righteous are defiled. My meaning is this: no soul can be at peace with God or have any fellowship with the Lord, without in some measure being sanctified and made holy. For God cannot make His residence in a soul that is always a stinking dunghill, and therefore of necessity it must be sanctified. One corner or other of the soul must be made so clean that the Lord of heaven, by His Holy Spirit, may make His residence in it. Now let us see how the heart is sanctified. Peter says that the soul of man is purified by faith, that the heart of man is purged by faith (Acts 15:9). Therefore faith in Christ Jesus opens and purges the heart, and in the merit of His Blood we have peace with God. As the Apostle says, 'being justified by faith, we have peace with God through our Lord Jesus Christ' (Rom. 5:1).

Now we come to a further point, that you have to prove yourselves, whether you are in the faith or not, as the Apostle says (2 Cor. 13:5). Examine your soul to see if it is seasoned with this faith, for if you do not have faith in Christ, Christ is not in you, and if Christ is not in you, then you are in an evil state, in the state of the reprobate and the condemned. Therefore everyone ought to look carefully and see if he has a belief in the love of Christ or not, whether or not he believes that he obtains mercy by His merits, and sanctification by His Blood. If you have no measure of this faith, you have no measure of peace with God, for peace with God is engendered and grows daily more and more by true faith in Christ. Now where this faith is true, where it is lively, and unites the heart with God, as I have already said, it must break out in word and deed; it cannot be held in. It must break out in word, glorifying the God of heaven, who has forgiven us our sins; it must break forth in word by giving a notable confession of those sins wherein we have offended Him. It must break out in deed in doing good works, to testify to the world that which is in your heart, to testify to the world that you who have this faith are a new person, that by your good example of life and conversation, you may edify your brothers and sisters, the simple ones of the Church of God, and by your holy life you may draw sinners to repentance, that they, seeing your life, may be compelled to glorify God in you.

[1] The first point in which to try yourself is, to look to the heart, the mouth and the hand. See that there is harmony among these three, that they all sing one song. If the heart is inwardly united to God, there is no doubt but that the mouth will outwardly glorify Him, and if

your heart and mouth are renewed, and are at one, then of necessity you must express this in your conversation. There must also be agreement between the heart and hand; your conversation must be changed along with the heart, and be wholly honest and godly, like it. Therefore if your conversation is good, it is a sure token that you are at one with God, but if your conversation is not good, say what you will, your heart is only defiled, and this true and lively faith has no place in it. If you ask, then, when you are one with God, the answer is, when your conversation, your heart and your mouth, all say one thing. Then, unquestionably, you have the work of faith wrought by the Holy Spirit in your heart, which makes you at peace with God. That is the first point in which you should try yourselves.

[2] The next point is love. You must try whether you are in love and charity with your neighbour, or not. As you are not united with God, except by the bond of faith, so you are not united with your neighbour, or joined with any member of Christ on this earth, except by the bond of love, amity and charity. Take away love, and you are not a member of His Body. For love is the master sinew which unites all these members of Christ's Body together, and makes them grow up in a spiritual and mystical unity. Love is the only mark by which the children of Christ and members of Christ's Body are known from the rest of the world. Love is the holy oil which refreshes our souls and makes us like God. The more we grow in love, the more God by His Spirit dwells in us, for God is love. Therefore unless in some measure love towards your neighbour dwells in your heart, you can have no fellowship with your neighbour, far less with God. If the behaviour of men were examined by

164

this rule, we should find a multitude of godless people in this country, who have hearts raging with malice against one another. Where the devil and a malicious spirit dwell, there is no place for the Holy Spirit. And now, even though the Lord has done everything possible to instruct them, to infuse into them this precious love and amity toward God and their neighbour, and so to alter their condition, yet they will not allow themselves to be awakened, until the great vengeance and malediction of God falls upon them. Nevertheless, this love, this honest and godly conversation, all flow from the root of faith, so that if your heart has faith in any measure, even if it be ever so small, in that same measure you must have love toward your neighbour. And this love is never idle, but is always expressing itself in some way or another. Because faith is the ground upon which all the rest depends, and because this faith is such a jewel, that without it, it is impossible for any of you to please God, without it all your deeds are an abomination before Him and without it you are left in a terrible misery (which is all the more terrible when you are ignorant of it), is there not good reason why you should know and understand how this faith is wrought and created in our souls by the Holy Spirit, and how it is maintained and nourished in us? Thus, when you see how it is created, and hear how it is brought about, you may examine your consciences, and see whether you are in the faith or not.

4. The Holy Spirit's work within us

I had intended to dwell upon this longer than the time now permits. Now, however, as time permits and God gives me grace, let me teach you how the Holy Spirit operates in the hearts and minds of men and women, and what pains He takes in creating and forming this precious faith in their souls. Yet before I embark upon that, it is necessary, and more than necessary, for you to understand your own misery and infirmity, and to know how the Lord came to recover you out of your former state, and to recreate you when you were lost by the deed of your forefather Adam.

We are children of the first Adam

In order to consider this matter more profoundly, I remind you of this fact, that man universally, and every man particularly, is corrupted and lost, and that by his first father's fault. Even if there were no more than that first fall and sin of Adam's, we would all be justly condemned to a double death, both of body and soul for ever. Since man is thus utterly lost, universally and particularly, without any hope of return left in his soul, without any sense of a recovery of that former state or repairing of the image which he lost to sin long before, and is left in this desperate condition in himself, what does God do? The ever-living God, the only wise God, whose ways are unsearchable, has found out a way how man, thus lost, may yet be saved. From whom did He seek counsel in this? Not from any creature, but from Himself. The three persons of the Trinity took counsel with themselves. The one God was moved to seek counsel from Himself, being moved by Himself alone, for He did not have any principle outside Himself to induce Him. What then did God do, when thus moved in Himself to act according to His own counsel (Eph. 1 :9)?

When all men and women should have died for ever, it pleased Him in His infinite mercy, to elect a certain number out of the lost race of Adam, whom He willed to be sanctified, justified and glorified. Therefore in order to accomplish the work of their salvation, He appointed His own proper Son (for He had but one Son), the second person of the Trinity, God, in power, glory and majesty as high as Himself, equal with God the Father in all things, He appointed Him to work this work, to bring about our redemption and eternal salvation. (This is but the mystery of it in some measure disclosed). And therefore in the fullness of time—for He dispenses all times according to His wisdom—at the time He appointed, He sent down His Son to possess Himself of the womb of the Virgin, to take on our flesh, to take on the likeness of sin. Sin itself He did not take on, but He did take on the likeness of sin. What do I mean by this *likeness of sin*? Our flesh is the likeness of sin. It was our flesh and nature that He assumed, but it was perfectly sanctified in the very moment of His conception in the womb of the Virgin.

The elect are made children of the second Adam

He took this flesh on Himself that in this flesh and nature, sin might be banished and cast out of us for ever. And whereas we should all have gone one way (for there is no exception of persons by nature), Christ Jesus our Saviour has elected us, and according as His Father in His secret election before the beginning of the world had elected us, so Christ Jesus in His own time calls us and makes us partakers of that salvation which He has purchased. He repairs not only that image which was lost in our forefather Adam, but He gives us a far more excellent image than we lost. He places us not in a terrestrial paradise, where Adam was placed in the beginning (and what more could have been sought by us?), but He places us in a higher and more celestial paradise than we lost. This paradise which He gives us is as much more heavenly as the Son of God, and God Himself, is far above any creature that ever was, man or angel. If we had remained in the image in which our forefather was created, we would have settled ourselves in the earth for ever, we should not have desired a better paradise than an earthly one for our dwelling. But now, through the kindness of the second Adam, Christ Jesus our Saviour, the Son of God, it comes to pass that we are raised up out of earth to heaven, and to a heavenly paradise. But what have we to do with heaven? Are we not made of earth, and made to return to the earth? Is not an earthly body fitted for an earthly paradise? Yet the Lord in His mercy sent down His Son to draw us up out of the earth to heaven.

This is so high a thing that it cannot be easily considered, for this drawing of us to a heavenly paradise is something transcending our thought. How could the heart of man come to think that we should live the life of angels in heaven? Yet this is what it has pleased the living Lord to do, in the great riches and compassion of His mercy, and in the exceeding greatness of His mercy toward us. (In the Epistle to the Ephesians, the Apostle cannot find sufficient words to express this; he hardly knows how to begin or how to end, when he speaks of the riches of that mercy. If you examine that Epistle carefully, you will find there more exalted and excellent ways of speaking of the riches of that mercy than anywhere else in Scripture.) It pleased Him, I say, not to give us simply the image that we lost, nor to leave us on this earth, but to give us a better image, and besides that, to place us in heaven, where we may remain with Him for ever.

The Spirit makes us sure of our redemption

Now does His mercy and grace stop here? No. In order that this salvation, which He has already procured and brought about by His Son, our Saviour Christ Jesus, may be wholly accomplished, with nothing lacking in it, He makes this same redemption come to our knowledge. As He has redeemed us in His own person purposely, so He makes us sure of it in our consciences. How does He do that? As by His death He purchased our full redemption, so He intimates and makes it known to us by our inward calling, letting us both find and feel in our hearts what He did for us in His Body. For when our Lord makes His servants intimate and proclaim this redemption to our consciences, He works this precious faith in our souls, which assures us that the Son of God has died for us. For what could it avail us to see our redemption, our salvation and our life afar off, if no way were found, and if no hand or means were given us by which to apprehend that salvation, and apply it to ourselves. What can it avail a sick man to see a drug in an apothecary's shop, unless a way is found of applying it to his sick body? Therefore in order that this work of our redemption and salvation may be fully and freely accomplished, as freely as He has given His only Son to death on the Cross for us, so freely has He found out this way and means and gifted us with this hand, whereby we may take hold of Christ, and apply Him to our souls.

To conclude, then, this means is faith. There is no way nor instrument in the Scriptures of God by which we can apply Christ to our souls, except faith. Therefore faith cannot be commended enough. Turn to faith, and it will make you turn to God; and so unite you with God, and make all your actions well-pleasing to Him.

Sola fide—by faith alone

There is no good action that we do, no matter how well it appears before the world, but it is abomination before God, and furthers our condemnation, if it is not done in faith. If we have faith, all the creatures of God must smile upon us; they must all conspire to further the work of our salvation. On the other hand, if we lack faith, all God's creatures will be our enemies, and conspire to our damnation. Faith conjoins us with the God of heaven, and makes us heavenly. This precious faith is mixed with all the gifts and graces which God gives us, all the riches of the earth are of no value to my soul without faith. And what does it avail for any man to have all the science, knowledge and wisdom in the world, without faith? For the devil has all this knowledge, and is none the better. What does it avail for me to conquer all the monarchies and kingdoms, and to possess all the riches on earth, what can all this avail for my soul? Nothing, but to make out a case against me, if I am devoid of faith. Therefore all the benefits and gifts of God without faith avail nothing but to augment our misery.

All the gifts and graces of God are abused without faith. Faith alone makes you use the benefits and graces of God rightly, faith alone should be sought, kept and entertained here in this life. If you have faith, all the rest of God's graces are profitable to you, for this jewel keeps them all in order, and makes them all fruitful, whereas without it, everything here on earth will only bear witness against you.

Then let us come to speak of this faith, and how it is created in the soul. I base my argument on John 6:44, where our Master says: 'No man can come to me except the Father which has sent me draw him.' In these words we see clearly that unless we are forcibly drawn and compelled, unless from being unwilling we are made willing by God the Father, it is not possible for us to come to His Son. Why is it that the Spirit of God must draw us, and make us willing before ever we come to God? Because by nature we are not only wounded and lanced by sin and iniquity, but as the Apostle shows, we are 'wholly dead in trespasses and sins' (Eph. 2:1). Moreover, see how void any dead body is of natural life—so void are our souls (even though they are alive with natural life) of the life of God, of that heavenly and spiritual life to which we aspire in this life, until the time when the Spirit of God draws, i.e. quickens our hearts and minds. This is not what we commonly mean by 'drawing'. It is rather the 'quickening' of something dead, of what is void of the life of the Spirit. Therefore unless the Spirit of God draws us, that is quickens us with that spiritual and heavenly life, it is impossible for us to go to heaven, and unless He nourishes that life which He has begun, it is impossible for us to continue in it. And so the Spirit of God is said to draw us, that is to begin this life in us, and by the same Holy Spirit to continue and nourish this life in us. Now by the drawing of the Spirit our souls are quickened, but by the drawing of the Spirit I understand nothing else than the forging and creating of faith in our souls, which makes us new creatures.

The order of the Spirit's work within us

[1] Now let us see what order the Spirit of God maintains in drawing us, and in forging and creating this faith in our souls. First of all I divide the soul into no more parts than commonly it is wont to be divided, that is, into the heart and the mind. Our mind is clouded in darkness, altogether blind naturally, with nothing in it but vanity and error, so that we vanish away and cannot continue long in any good purpose. What then does the Spirit of God do? (1) The first work that the Spirit of God does is *to bring order into the mind*: He banishes darkness, expels vanity and blindness, that naturally lurk in the mind, and instead of this darkness He puts within a celestial and heavenly light, a light which dwells in Christ Jesus only. Thus the Spirit drives away the cloud of mist and darkness and puts light into the mind. And what does He do with this light? (2) As soon as we get this inward light and a sanctified understanding, *He makes us see God*: not only as God the Creator of the world, but also as God the Redeemer, who has redeemed us in His Son, Christ Jesus.

Now, before I obtain this light, what are my heart and mind doing? Every one of you has experienced, as I myself have, in what state the heart and mind are before this light enters. The mind lies drowned in blindness, and the heart is hardened, and they both conspire together in one vice, to set up an idol, instead of God—a domestic and invisible idol. What sort of idol is this, I pray? No doubt some worldly or fleshly affection or other, set up on the throne of your heart, and on this idol you bestow the devotion of your whole heart and mind and soul and body, so that the devotion of your soul and body, which should be bestowed on God only, is bestowed upon that idol, set up in your heart, that is, in the place of God, instead of the Most High. And you are more addicted to the service of that idol than ever you were to the service of the living God. Indeed, until this idol is banished, and the blindness through which it is served is taken away, there is not one of you but is a servant to one lust or another; and your soul that should be consecrated to the service of the living God, is employed upon some affection or other, on some worldly or fleshly lust of your own.

But now from the time that the Lord begins to scatter the clouds of our natural mind and understanding, and begins to chase away the thick mist from the darkened soul, and to place in it some spark of heavenly light that comes from Christ, whereas we were children of the night and darkness before, (3) He now makes us to be light in the Lord, and children of the light, and of the day. Thus we see that all things in the world besides the living God are vanities, deceptive allurements, inconstant shadows, fleeting and flowing without any stability, and thus we see that our hearts and minds are set on evil continually. Then we begin to abhor that idol, and to seek to serve God only.

Now unless the Lord in His mercy and goodness, puts this light within us, and until we get some glimmering of this light, we can never see our own vanity, far less see God. This then is the first work of the Spirit. He banishes darkness and error, and brings light into our minds. Now this first work of the Spirit is often expressed in the Scripture under the name of faith, for the mind has its own assent and persuasion, according to its own nature, as well as the heart. And therefore when the mind is enlightened and conditioned by this light, its assent and knowledge is called faith. The Apostles and Evangelists give to this knowledge the name of faith, for as soon as you have an eye for God and Christ Jesus, whom He has sent, as soon as you have sight of Him, and gain access to Him, even if it were only in the mind, it is called faith.

[2] But we are forbidden to stop here. If faith goes no farther than the mind, it is not the faith that we are seeking. For the faith that justifies and does us good, must open the heart as well as the mind; it must banish that idol and affection out of the heart, and in its place put a throne for Christ Jesus. Thus, unless the good Spirit of God goes farther than the mind, and banishes this idol out of the heart as well as out of the mind, we do not have that justifying faith whereby we look for mercy. *The Spirit of God must not only enlighten the mind, but it must mollify this heart of yours, and change your affections.* And whereas your affections were wicked and evil, God's Spirit must change the will, and He can never change the will unless He makes the ground of your heart good, that it may be set on God, and bring forth fruit abundantly to its owner.

What does this teach us? This teaches you to seek for an honest heart, and to seek earnestly until you obtain it. For what does it avail for a man to know what is good or evil, unless he is shown how he may eschew the evil, and unless he is given the means to make him a partaker of the good? Is not this a useless and unprofitable knowledge for me to see afar off and to know that this is good for me, when I do not find any way of being a partaker of it, so that it may be of special benefit to me? Is it not a useless knowledge also to perceive that this is bad for me, that it will do me hurt if I do it, when nevertheless I do that very thing, and no other? So the Spirit of God links these two together in this work: as He reforms the mind, He reforms also the heart, and makes you to be partakers of the good that you see, and to eschew the evil.

This is the second work of the Spirit, not only to present a thing to you, but actually to make it yours. For even if the mind does its part ever so well, and shows you that Christ is yours, and presents Him to you ever so often, nevertheless if your heart is not reformed, the evil and crooked affection that is in your heart will prefer itself to Christ, and will make you account everything but folly in comparison with it. Therefore it would be a useless and foolish thing for me to see my salvation unless I were given grace to partake of it. What does it avail you to see the devil, to see your own sins that slay you, unless you are given grace to eschew them? And so the second work of the Spirit is this: He enters into the heart, subdues and wonderfully changes it, and makes the will obedient; He mollifies the affection that was hard before, in such a way that you are made to pour out your affection in some measure on the living God, whereas before it was poured out on some idol or other of your own. Thus unless the heart does its part, as the mind does, the whole soul is not consecrated to God, for God has not made the soul in such a way that the heart should serve you, but that the mind only should serve Him. Your service is only then acceptable to God when you consecrate your heart as well as your mind to Him.

Now this matter is so clear that it does not need to be illustrated, yet in order to make it more plain to you, I shall show you by a similitude that the apprehension of the mind is not enough, without the apprehension of the heart as well. In corporal things, in meat and drink, which are for the use of your body, there must be two kinds of apprehension; so there are also two kinds of apprehension of the Body and Blood of Christ Jesus, which are our spiritual meat and drink. For corporal meat and drink there is one apprehension, by the eye and the taste: when the meat is present to you on the table, your eye views and discerns it and chooses it; and not only the eye, for the taste also discerns the meat, and approves it—that is called the *first* apprehension.

Now the *second* apprehension follows from this. After you have chewed the meat, swallowed it and sent it to your stomach, where it is digested and converted into your nourishment, then in your stomach you get the second apprehension. But if you do not like or taste that meat, the second apprehension does not follow, for you will spit it out again, or reject it. preferring some other meat that you like better. The meat that you do not like, never enters your stomach, and so it can never be converted into your nourishment. For it is only the second apprehension of the meat that brings nourishment to the body in our corporal food. Therefore if you do not chew this meat and swallow it, it does not feed you. It is only the second apprehension that nourishes our bodies.

The case is similar with spiritual things, so far as they may be compared in this way. In regard to the food of Christ Jesus, who is the life and nurture of our souls and consciences, there must be two kinds of apprehension. (1) The first is by the eye of the mind, that is, by our knowledge and understanding: for as the eye of the body discerns by an outward light, so the eye of the mind discerns by an inward and renewed understanding, whereby we get our first apprehension of Christ. Now if this first apprehension of Christ pleases us well, then the next follows. (2) We then begin to set the affection of our hearts on Him, we have good will towards Him, for all our affections proceed from our will, and when our affections are renewed and made holy, we set them wholly upon Christ. We love Him, and if we love Him, we take hold of Him, eat Him and digest Him, that is, we apply Him to our souls, and so from our loving and desiring Him, our second apprehension of Him follows.

But if we have no will towards Him, if we have no love nor desire for Him, what do we do? We reject Him, and prefer our own idol, and the service of our own affections, to Him. And the second apprehension does not follow. We cannot digest Him, and if we cannot digest Him, the spiritual life cannot grow in us. For the service which your eye renders to your body is the same as that which your knowledge and understanding render to your soul, and the service your hand, your mouth, your taste and your stomach render to your body, is the same that your heart and affections render to your soul. Therefore as our bodies cannot be nourished unless our hands take and our mouths eat the meat, from which the second apprehension may follow, so likewise our souls cannot feed on Christ unless we lay hold of Him, and embrace Him heartily by our will and affection. For we do not come to Christ by any outward motion of our bodies, but by an inward motion and apprehension of the heart. For God, finding us all in a reprobate condition, brings us to Christ by reforming the affection of our soul, and by making us love Him. Therefore the second apprehension by which we digest our Saviour, will never take place in our souls unless He pleases the eye, and so pleases the will and affection as well. Now if it comes to pass that our wills and affections are wholly bent upon Christ, then no doubt we have gained this jewel of faith. Do you have such a liking in your minds, and such a love in your hearts for Christ, that you will prefer Him before all things in the world? Then without doubt faith is begun in you.

[3] Now when a thing is begun, more is required, for though this faith is formed in your minds, in your hearts and souls, yet that is not enough. *That which is formed must be nourished.* He who is conceived must be entertained and brought up. Thus unless the love that is begun in me by the Holy Spirit is daily entertained and nourished by ordinary means, it will decay. Unless the Lord continues to draw me to Him through the working of His Holy Spirit, it is impossible for me to continue in the faith.

How are we to nourish and continue faith in our souls? In two ways. (1) First we must nourish faith begun in our souls by hearing the Word, not every word, but by hearing the Word of God preached, and not by hearing every man, but by hearing the Word preached by him who is sent. For this is the ordinary means by which the Lord has bound Himself, He works faith through the hearing of the Word, and (2) the receiving of the Sacraments. And the more you hear the Word, and the oftener you receive the Sacraments, the more your faith is nourished. Now it is not only by hearing the Word, and receiving the Sacraments, that we nourish faith. The Word and Sacraments are not able of themselves to nourish this faith in us, unless the working of the Holy Spirit is conjoined with their ministry. But the Word and Sacraments are said to nourish faith in our souls because they offer and exhibit Christ to us, who is the meat, drink and life of our souls. Because in the Word and Sacraments we get Christ who is the food of our souls, the Word and Sacraments are said to nourish our souls. Thus it is said of the disciples of Christ that 'they continued in the Apostles' doctrine and fellowship and breaking of bread and prayers' (Acts 2:42). In this way they entertained, augmented and nourished the faith that was begun in them. Thus the Holy Spirit begets this faith, works and creates it, nourishes and entertains it in our soul, through the hearing of the Word, and through participation in the Sacraments. They are the ordinary means by which the Lord nourishes us, and continues to give us spiritual food. Therefore the spiritual life is nourished and entertained by the same means as it is begun, as our temporal life is entertained and nourished by the same means by which it is begun.

Seeing therefore that by these means the Holy Spirit begets this work of faith in our souls, it is our duty to pray that He may continue the work which He has begun, for this cause we should resort to the hearing of the Word when it is preached, and to the receiving of the Sacraments when they are ministered, that we may be fed in our souls to life everlasting. But alas! we have come to such a loathing, disdain, and rejection of this heavenly food, in this country, that where men in the beginning would have gone some twenty miles, some forty miles to the hearing of the Word, they will now scarcely come from their houses to the Church, and remain one hour to hear the Word, but rather abide at home. Well, I say, too much wealth turns the head, and the abundance of this Word engenders such a dislike that it is a rare thing to find any that thirst and desire to hear the Word as they were wont to do in the beginning. And as for our great men, they will not hear it at all, for they cannot endure to hear the thing that accuses them and convicts them. Therefore they run away from it, but they should not do so; they should not shun Christ or His Word. They should rather hear the Word, and as the Word accuses them, they should accuse themselves also, that thereby they may come to a confession of their sin, and obtain mercy for it.

Therefore when Christ accuses you, you should not run away from Him, but draw near to Him, you should claim kinship and inheritance in Him, and so, as it were, break into and forcibly enter into His kingdom. It is not the way when your sins touch you and when Christ accuses you, to run away from Him. No, you should turn to Him. You should confess your sin, cry 'peccavi' (I have sinned), and seek mercy. And after you have received mercy, this Word will become as pleasant to you and you will take as great delight in coming to hear it, as ever you did in fleeing from it before. But alas! our dislike and disdain have grown to such a height that truly I am moved to believe firmly that the Lord has concluded that we shall not enter into His rest if only because of this great contempt for His mercy and grace, which are now so richly offered to us. God cannot deal otherwise with us than He dealt with our forefathers, the

Israelites, for the neglect of the Evangel, which in their day was only preached obscurely, for then it was far from the incarnation of Christ—and the farther it was from His incarnation, the more obscurely was the Word preached, under dark types and shadows. Notwithstanding the fathers that heard the Evangel preached and did not believe, all perished in the wilderness except two, as you have heard before from this place. If they perished for contempt of so dark a light, much more must you, who are their children, perish, for contempt of the Sun of righteousness who has risen so plainly and shines so clearly now in the preaching of the Gospel —that is, unless the Lord in His mercy anticipates you, and unless you anticipate His judgements by earnest seeking, and unless you seek an inward feeling and understanding through which you may see and feel the grace that is offered. Pray again that He will sanctify your heart by repentance, that you may repent of your sins, and lead an honest and godly life for all time to come, that both body and soul may be saved in the day of the Lord. The Lord work this in your soul, that you may seek His mercy; and in seeking mercy may obtain it, and in mercy may lay hold of Christ, for the sake of His righteous merit. To whom with the Father and the Holy Spirit be all honour, praise, and glory, now and for ever. Amen.

5

THE PREPARATION FOR THE
LORD'S SUPPER 2

*Let every man therefore examine himself, and so let him eat
of this bread, and drink of this cup.*

1 CORINTHIANS 11:28.

IN the doctrine of our trial and due examination, the
Apostle, as you have heard, dearly beloved in Christ
Jesus, gave us a special command that every one of us
should try and examine himself strictly, that is, every
man should humbly enter into his own conscience,
scrutinizing it to see in what state he finds it with God
and with his neighbour. He enjoins this trial upon us
and commands every one of us to take pains over the
true examination of his conscience. Why? Because no
one knows so much of me as I do myself; because no
man can be sure of the state of my conscience, but I
myself; and because no man can try my conscience as
diligently and as profitably as I myself. Therefore it is
fitting above all that all men and women, before they
enter into the hearing of the Word, before they give their
ear to the Word, or their mouth to the Sacrament,
should try and examine their own consciences. It is not
that the Apostle wishes to exclude other men from this
trial, for as it is lawful for me to try myself, so no doubt
it is lawful for my Pastor to try me. It is lawful for other
men, who have a care over me, to try and examine me;

but no man can do this so profitably to me as I myself. And even if we have ever so many triers and examiners, all is lost if we do not try ourselves. Whether there be a second or a third trier or not, each of us must be one, and the first of them. No doubt the Apostle's intention was to teach us clearly that he who comes to this Table without that knowledge or ability to try himself, is a profane communicant, and comes uncleanly. He comes only to his own destruction. Let every man therefore grow in knowledge, in understanding and in the Spirit, that he may be the more able to try and examine his own conscience.

In order that you may go forward and proceed in the work of this trial, with greater speed and with better fruits, we laid down the following order for this examination. First of all, I showed what it is which we call a conscience, and what is meant by it. Next, I gave the reasons why you should put your consciences to this trial, and strict examination. And thirdly, as far as time permitted, I entered into the points in which every one of you should try and examine your own conscience. In regard to the *conscience*, let me remind you again of its definition. *We call conscience a certain feeling in the heart resembling the righteous judgement of God, following upon a deed done by us, and flowing from a knowledge in the mind, a feeling accompanied by a motion in the heart, of fear or joy, of trembling or rejoicing.* I leave the development of these points to your memories, and pray God that they may be well

I dealt next with the *reasons* why every one of you should be careful in trying and examining your own conscience. *First*, because the Lord of heaven has His eye continually upon the conscience, for the eye of God is never off the conscience and heart of man, as I proved to you from several different passages. *Secondly*, because this God has chosen His lodging and has set down His throne and made His residence in the conscience. Therefore in order that He may dwell in cleanness, you ought to have regard for His dwelling place. *Thirdly*, He is the Lord, indeed the only Lord of your conscience, who alone has power to control, to save, or to cast away. Therefore in order that it may do good service to your own Lord, you ought to pay attention to your conscience. And *finally*, because the health of your soul depends on the state of your conscience, so that if your soul is in good health, your body cannot be evil, therefore because soul and body depend upon the state of the conscience, every one of you should carefully look to your conscience. I will not amplify this, but leave it to your memory to recall how the health and welfare of the soul should be preserved.

Next, I came in the third and last place to the *points* in which every one of you should try and examine your conscience. As you may remember, I set down two points in which you ought to put your consciences to the test: *first*, as to whether your conscience was at peace with God or not; *second*, as to whether your conscience was in love, in charity and in amity with your neighbour or not. It is chiefly in regard to these two points that you must try and examine yourselves. To know whether you are at peace with God or nor, you must first try, as the Apostle says, whether you are in the faith of Christ or not; for if you are in the faith, and are thereby justified, you must of necessity have peace with God. Therefore the next thing you must do is to try your faith, to see whether you have faith or not. Faith can only be tried by its fruits. It can only be viewed and judged by its effects. Therefore in order to try whether you are in the faith or not, note the fruits, take heed to your mouth, to your hands and to your deeds, for unless you glorify God with your mouth, and confess your salvation, and unless you glorify Him also in your deeds, and make your holy life a witness to your holy faith, all is but vanity and mere hypocrisy.

Thus, to know the sincerity of your faith, you must see that there is harmony between your hand, your mouth and your heart, that there is a mutual consent between them, in which neither your action nor your mouth prejudges your heart, but your mouth and hand together testify to the sincerity of your heart. If the heart, hand and mouth consent and agree in harmony together, then unquestionably the heart that yields such good fruit is united with God. Thus the light of your deeds, the shining of your life, will glorify the name of your God.

It is evident, then, that the whole weight of our trial depends principally on this point, in seeing whether we have faith, in examining whether Christ dwells in us by faith or not. For without faith there can be no union or conjunction between us and Christ; without faith our hearts cannot be sanctified and cleansed, and without faith we cannot work by charity. Thus everything depends upon this alone. And therefore in order that you might understand better whether you have faith or not, I went more deeply into this matter, and began to show you how the Holy Spirit creates faith in your souls, hearts and minds. I began to show you what order the Holy Spirit keeps forming and creating this notable instrument in your hearts and minds, not only how He engenders and begins faith, but also how He entertains and nourishes it; and I showed you also the external means and instruments which He uses to this effect.

To beget faith in our souls, the Holy Spirit uses the hearing of the Word preached by him who is sent, and the ministry of the Sacraments, as ordinary means and instruments. These are only effectual when the Holy Spirit concurs inwardly in our hearts with the Word striking outwardly on our ear, and with the Sacrament outwardly received. Unless the Holy Spirit grants His concurrence to the Word and Sacrament, Word and Sacrament will not produce faith. Everything depends, then, upon the operation of the Holy Spirit; the whole regeneration of mankind, the renewing of the heart and of the conscience, depend on the power of the Holy Spirit; and therefore it behoves us carefully to employ our labours in calling upon God for His Holy Spirit. It is by this means and no other that the Holy Spirit begets faith in us, and nourishes and augments what He has already begotten. And therefore as we get faith by the hearing of the Word, so by continual and diligent hearing we have this faith augmented and nourished in us. And here I draw out my exhortation: if you would have spiritual life nourished in you, and if you would have further assurance of heaven, you must of necessity hear the blessed Word of God continually and diligently.

Personal application of the doctrine

Now it remains for every one of you carefully to apply this doctrine to your own soul, and to scrutinize your own conscience to see if this faith is begun in your heart and mind or not. Let us now examine together how far or how little the Holy Spirit has proceeded in this work.

Has a change taken place in your mind?

The first effect of the Holy Spirit according to which you may try your mind to see whether you are in the faith or not, is discerned thus: turn over your memories and recall if at any time it has pleased the Lord in His mercy to turn the darkness of your mind into light, to remove from you the darkness which prevented you from seeing what you were by nature, or from seeing God in Christ, or any part of His mercy. Examine, I say, whether this darkness of the natural understanding is turned into light by the working of the Spirit or not. If you are become a child of the light, a child of the day, if you are become, as the Apostle says, 'light in the Lord', if a change has taken place in your mind, which before was closed up by nature in darkness and blindness and filled with vanity and errors, if the Lord has at any time enlightened the eye of your mind and made you see your own misery, the ugliness of your own nature, and the heinous sins which beset you by nature, if He has granted to you an insight into yourself, if He has also granted you a way of deliverance, an insight into the mercy of God in Christ Jesus, and if you have gained such a vision of the riches of His grace in Christ, *then* no doubt the Holy Spirit has begun a good work in you, which will bring forth repentance and which He will perfect in His own time. Therefore this is the first thing that must engage your attention, the first point in which you ought to examine your mind, to see if any light is there, by means of which you may know your misery, and have an insight into the mercy of God in Christ.

Is your heart also reformed and your will obedient?

If you do find a vision of these two in your mind, then go from your mind into your heart, and as you have tried your mind, try your heart also. And first, examine your heart to see whether or not it is so changed and reformed that its will is framed and bowed to God's obedience, its affection turned into the love of God, and poured out on Him as it was on vanities, on filthiness, and on the world before. Test your heart to see whether the ground and the source from which your motions and affections proceed, is sanctified or not. For from a holy fountain, holy waters distil; from a holy fountain, holy motions, holy thoughts and sanctified considerations must flow.

Then try and examine your heart to see if the Spirit of God has wrought such a reformation in it or not. And in order that you may better understand the working of the Holy Spirit, in your conscience and heart, (in which He chiefly resides), I shall explain to you the first fruits that the Holy Spirit brings forth in the heart, in framing, mollifying and bowing it to the obedience of God. You can recognise the working of the Holy Spirit through this effect, namely, if your mind sees and beholds what is good, sees and beholds your own misery, and the sins which cast you into it, and sees and beholds also the riches of the mercy of God in Christ, if as your mind sees these two, your heart is reformed and prepared to love the sight of the mercy of God in Christ, if you have a heart to desire mercy, a thirst and earnest desire to partake of it, then where this desire and thirst are, there the Holy Spirit is, and He has without doubt opened up your heart. Moreover, if as you see His mercy you see your own misery, if as your mind sees your misery, it also sees the fountain from which your misery flows, i.e. from your own sin, and if your heart hates this, then unquestionably the Holy Spirit is there. And if as you hate it, you also sorrow for it (for it is not enough to hate sin if you do not lament committing it), and with a godly sorrow deplore it, then the Holy Spirit is there. And again, if with your lamenting you are careful and eager to avoid that sin, then the Holy Spirit is there. (For what does it avail to lament if like a dog returning to its vomit you fall into the same pit again?) Therefore wherever there is a hatred and sorrow for sin, care and resolve to avoid it, without doubt the Holy Spirit has opened your heart, and is working out that precious instrument.

Examine your heart, then, according to all this operation of the Holy Spirit, see and perceive if the Holy Spirit has entered so deeply into you as to produce in that hard heart of yours an earnest and diligent desire, a careful solicitude continually to be reconciled with the great God whom you have offended. Is there such a thing as a thirst and a desire to be at amity with the God of heaven whom you have offended by your manifold transgressions? Where this earnest desire and thirst for reconciliation are in the heart, without doubt the heart is sincerely content not only to renounce sin, and all the impieties that separated you from God, but if endued with this thirst, it will sincerely renounce itself and, stubborn as it was before, cast itself down at the feet of Almighty God, and be wholly content to be ruled for ever by His holy Will. It will refuse to follow its own lust, its own will and appetite, as it did before, but will resign itself wholly into the hands of Almighty God, to be ruled by His Will, and to obey His commands. And unless you find this disposition in your heart, to quit and renounce yourself, it is vain for you to say that you thirst to be reconciled to God. Therefore the greater my thirst for reconciliation, the more my desire grows, and the more the apprehension of my misery, of the deep gulfs and hells to which my soul is subject, increases in my soul, the more earnest am I in being reconciled to God. To be reconciled I would not hesitate to renounce the lusts of my heart. I would even renounce my heart itself, and obedience to its will and desire, because I see I must die for ever, because I see the great deeps and oceans of all misery into which I shall fall at the end unless the Lord in His mercy reconciles Himself with me. To escape these deeps and calamities, can there be any doubt that the heart that is conscious of them, and moved by them, will most willingly renounce itself?

And again, since the Lord has taken pains to deliver me out of that deep misery in which I had drowned myself, and has purchased my redemption with so costly a price, not with gold or silver, or with any dross of the earth, but in a way so wonderful, by such a precious price and rich ransom, and so when we look to the greatness of our misery, and to the greatness of the price by which He has redeemed us, what heart is there but would willingly renounce itself to share in that redemption and be delivered out of that hell in which we are engulfed, and in which we will be in greater measure hereafter, unless we are reconciled to God? So then along with this choice there is joined a disposition in the heart in which the heart is willing in some measure to renounce itself. This lesson is often taught us by Christ in His Gospel: we must take up the cross and renounce ourselves before we can follow Him. The more this thirst grows in the heart, the more does this renunciation of ourselves grow also. On the other hand, the more this thirst decays and diminishes in the heart, and the more we cleave to the world and to the flesh, the more are we ruled and guided by them. Thus either we must nourish a hunger for life everlasting, a thirst for mercy, and a hunger after the righteousness that is in Christ, or else it will be impossible for us in any way to be His disciples.

Peace and a foretaste of heaven

Now to proceed: the heart that is thus prepared, that is, disposed to be reconciled and ready to renounce itself is never frustrated of its expectation, and is never disappointed. But as the Lord has imprinted in it an earnest desire to be reconciled, and to lay hold on Christ, so He puts that heart in some measure in possession of the mercy which it seeks, in possession of Christ Jesus Himself. This apprehension of Christ the heart feels and grasps with certainty in that peace which He gives to the conscience. Thus the conscience which was previously terrified, exceedingly gnawed and distracted, is quieted and pacified at once by the entry of this peace and of Christ with His graces. A calmness and soundness comes into the heart, and all troubles and storms are removed.

With this peace there is conjoined a taste of the powers of the world to come. The heart gets a taste of the sweetness that is in Christ, of the joy that is in the life everlasting, which is only the earnest of that full and

191

perfect joy into which soul and body will enter in that life. As you know, earnest money [a deposit paid in advance] must be not only a part of the whole sum, but an advance payment in the same kind. And therefore this earnest of joy assures us that when we shall get possession of the whole sum, it will be a wondrous joy. These pledges lift up the heart and keep it from lingering or being weary in the expectation of that life. They keep refreshing us from time to time, as through the frequent giving of earnest money, and assure us of the full fruition of that joy for which in patience we shall sustain all trouble. Therefore as the Holy Spirit works in us a thirst for Christ, for mercy and reconciliation with Him, so the same Holy Spirit does not disappoint that expectation, but puts the soul and heart in possession of Christ. In this way the conscience is pacified, the heart is rejoiced, and we get a taste of the sweetness and of the powers of the life to come.

What is it that the evident feeling of this taste, that passes all understanding, does in my heart and conscience? *It works a wonderful assurance and persuasion that God loves me.* The feeling of His mercy in the depth of my heart, in the bottom of my conscience, works a certain assurance and persuasion that He is my God, that He will save me for Christ's sake, and that the promise of mercy which for the life of me I did not dare to apply before to my conscience, now by the feeling of His mercy I dare apply boldly and say, 'Mercy pertains to me; life and salvation belong to me!'

Faith and assurance grow

When the conscience is exceedingly terrified and sees nothing in God but fire and wrath, it is not possible for it to do anything but to flee from Him. It cannot approach a consuming fire. But from the time that the conscience gets a taste of this peace, mercy and sweetness, as fast as it ever fled from God before, now after this reconciliation it runs to Him, and desires to possess Him more and more fully. Thus the assurance and persuasion of mercy arises from the feeling of mercy in the heart and conscience. Unless the heart feels and tastes it in some real measure, for the life of me I dare not apply God and His mercy to myself—nor does my conscience dare do so either. I may be sure in general that all my sins are remissible, and that I may obtain mercy, before I feel it. But I do not dare to apply this mercy particularly to myself until I feel a taste of it. Therefore this particular application whereby we claim God and Christ as our own, as if no one were entitled to Him but we, and so call Him *my* God, *my* Christ, and to claim His promises as if no one had an interest in them but we, all this is born of the conviction and feeling of mercy in the heart. The more this feeling grows, and the deeper the experience of this peace and mercy we have in our own heart, the stronger do our faith and assurance grow. Our persuasion becomes so strong that we dare at last to say with the Apostle: 'Who shall separate us from the love of Christ? Neither death nor life, nor angels nor principalities nor powers, nor things present, nor things to come, shall be able to separate us from the love of God which is in Christ Jesus our Lord' (Rom. 8:35, 38).

This particular application which arises no doubt from the feeling and conviction of divine mercy, is the specific difference, the chief mark and proper note whereby our faith (i.e. for us who are justified in the Blood of Christ) is distinguished from the general faith of the Papists. By this particular application our faith is not only distinguished from the general faith of the Papists, but from all the pretended faiths of all the sects in the world. For the Papist does not dare to apply the promise of mercy to his own soul; he accounts it presumption to say, 'I am elect, I am saved and justified'. And where does this come from? Only from the fact that in their conscience they have never felt mercy, they have never tasted of the love, favour and sweetness of God. For see, as fast as the conscience flees from God, before it gets any taste of His sweetness, so now it runs just as diligently to Him and presses its love upon Him. Thus they, miserable people, content themselves with this general faith, which is nothing else than a historical faith, i.e. one that rests only on the truth of God, and by which we know that the promises of God are true. But the Papist does not dare to come and say, 'These promises are true *in me*'. Why? Because he has not felt it, and his heart is not opened. But our justifying faith, as I told you, consecrates the whole soul to the obedience of God in Christ. Therefore it rests not only upon the truth of God, or upon the power of God (though these are two chief pillars of our faith also), but especially and chiefly upon the promise of grace and mercy in Christ. The soul of the Papist being destitute of the feeling and taste of mercy, does not dare to engage in this particular application, and so he cannot be justified. Doubtless, however, those of them who are justified in the mercy of God do get a taste of His kindness before they die. So much for the effects.

Then you have only this to remember: the opening of the heart, the pacifying and quieting of the conscience, produce an assurance and strong persuasion of the mercy of God in Christ. The more the heart is opened, the more the conscience is pacified, the more the taste of that sweetness continues and remains, the more are you assured of God's mercy. So then if you want to know whether your faith is strong or not, whether your persuasion of God's mercy is sure or not, look at your conscience. If your conscience is wounded [by some sin], assuredly you will doubt, and if you doubt, you cannot have such a strong persuasion as otherwise you would have if your doubting were removed. I do not mean that faith can be so perfect in this life that there will never be any doubt along with it. I do not claim such perfection, but I do say that a wounded conscience must always doubt, and the more we doubt, the less is our persuasion. Therefore the more you wound your conscience, the less faith you will have. And so you must come to this point: preserve a sound conscience, entertain peace in it, and you will preserve faith, and will have persuasion in the same proportion as you have rest and peace in your conscience. The more your conscience is at rest, the greater will your faith and persuasion be.

Preserve a good conscience

This argument, then, is sound: a doubting conscience causes weak faith, and the more doubt there is in your conscience, the weaker is your faith. Thus the Apostle does not lie when he says that faith dwells, is locked and closed up in a good conscience. Therefore if you preserve a good conscience, you will preserve a strong faith, and if you wound [sin against] your conscience, you will wound your faith. Now to make this more sure, how can I be persuaded of His mercy, whose anger I feel kindled against me, and against whom my conscience shows me that I am guilty of many offences? Certainly as long as the sense of His anger and the feeling of my offences remain, I cannot have a strong persuasion that He will be merciful to me. But when I gain access to His countenance, and see that He has forgiven me, then I begin to be persuaded. So then keep a good conscience, and you will keep your faith, and the better your conscience is, the stronger will your faith be.

To aristocrats, judges, advocates and merchants

The whole exhortation that we gather from this fact depends upon this, that every one of you, to whatever rank you belong, take heed to your conscience, for in losing it you lose your faith, and in losing your faith you lose [your hold on] salvation. Do you belong to the ranks of great men? You ought to take heed to your conscience, especially since the Lord has placed you in a great calling. You have many things in which you ought to control your conscience and consult it before you put your hand to any work, because you are bound in manifold duties to God and to your inferiors.

No doubt if some of our great men had taken care to consult their consciences, such degeneration would not have come upon their own bodies. This oppression of the poor, these deadly feuds with men of their own rank, would not have broken out so vehemently. But the Lord, seeing them take so little heed to their consciences, deprives them of faith, and of the hope of mercy, and their end will certainly be miserable. You who have eyes to behold will see the God of heaven make those men, who live so dissolutely, become spectacles of His judgements before the world, for the Lord does not leave

196

such men unpunished. From their example it is very necessary that men of inferior rank should take heed to their consciences, and therefore let every man, according to his calling, examine himself by the rule of his conscience.

Especially is it fitting that you, who are judges, before you pronounce and give judgement, should consult your own conscience, and its law. For in giving judgement you ought not to follow your inclination, but the rule of your conscience. Likewise, you who are of inferior rank to judges, and you who are advocates, ought to control your actions by your conscience. Do not give the lieges or subjects of this country just cause to complain of you. Do not frighten them from the pleading of justice by exorbitant fees, and extraordinary ways of behaviour, but moderate all your actions so that they agree with the rule of your conscience, in order that as far as it lies in you, justice will not cease.

What I say to them I say also to you of the merchant class. See that you do not look to this or that so much as to the conscience that is in you, considering according to the measure of knowledge God has given you, what you may do in accordance with your conscience, and whatever you do, beware of acting against your knowledge. I grant that your knowledge will not be so learned as it should be, and this accounts for many deformed actions. Nevertheless, let no man act against his knowledge, but let every man act according to the measure of the knowledge with which God has endued him, and even if he is not well informed, let him not do anything by guess, but consult his conscience and follow his knowledge, for whatever is done doubtingly is sin. Therefore whatever you do, do not let your eye, your hand, or any member of your body, act against your knowledge, for that would be a step toward that high sin against the Holy Ghost. This is a sure way to put all knowledge out of your minds, for if men act against knowledge, and continue to do so, at last they will become engulfed in darkness; the Lord will scrape all knowledge out of their minds, and all feeling of mercy out of their hearts. Therefore let every one of you follow his knowledge, and according to the measure of your knowledge let your actions be undertaken.

A precious gift to undeserving sinners

It has pleased the Lord to pour this wine, this precious ointment, into us. Even though we are frail earthen vessels, miserable creatures, yet it has pleased our gracious God to pour such a precious wine into our hearts and minds, and to entrust so precious a faith to our keeping, that by virtue of it we may take hold of Christ, who is our justice, wisdom, sanctification and redemption. Even though we are miserable creatures, yet the Lord in His mercy has a regard for us in Christ, in giving us this precious gift whereby our souls are fitted for life everlasting. In that He pours it into our hearts, we see clearly that it does not grow in our hearts, or breed in our nature. No, this gift of faith is not at man's command, or under his arbitrament, as if it lay in his power to believe or not to believe, as he pleases. It is the gift of God poured down freely from His undeserved grace in the riches of His mercy in Christ.

How can we know we have the gift of faith?

That it is a gift you see clearly from the words of the Apostle: 'And to another is given faith by the same

198

Spirit' (1 Cor. 12:9). And again, 'For unto you it is given in the behalf of Christ not only to believe on Him, but also to suffer for His sake' (Phil. 1:29). Thus faith is the gift of the Holy Spirit, but this gift is not given to all, as the Apostle plainly declares, 'All men have not faith' (2 Thess. 3:2). This gift is not given to all, but only to the elect, that is, to as many as the Lord has appointed to life everlasting. Wherever it is, and in whatever heart it is found, this gift is never idle, but is perpetually working, and it works well by love and charity, as the Apostle affirms (Gal. 5:6). And as the Apostle James testifies in his second chapter, wherever this gift is found, it is not dead, but living and vibrant. *There is no better way of learning whether it is lively and working or not, than to look at the fruit and effects that flow from it,* and therefore in order that you may be more assured of the goodness of your faith through its effects in you, I shall give you three special effects to observe, according to which you may judge it.

[1] *First* of all, look to your heart and scrutinize it. If you have a desire to ask God's mercy for your sins, to call upon His Holy Name for mercy and grace, *if there is such a thing in your heart as a desire to pray*, indeed if any part of your heart is inclined or has a thirst for mercy and grace, even though the greater part of your heart frets and would draw you away from prayer, nevertheless the desire to pray that you do have in any measure at all, is assuredly the true effect of genuine faith. If you have a heart to pray to God, even though this desire is but slender, assure yourself that your soul has life, for prayer is the life of your soul, and makes your faith lively. Why is that? Prayer is God's own gift; it is no gift of ours, for if it were ours, it would be evil.

But prayer is the best gift that God has ever given to man, and so it must be the gift of His own Holy Spirit, and being His gift, it makes our faith vibrant. Without this you are not able and you do not dare to call upon Him in whom you do not believe, as the Apostle says (Rom. 10:14). For if I entreat Him by prayer, I must trust in Him. Therefore prayer is a sure evidence of justifying faith and belief in God. For I cannot speak to Him, much less pray to Him, in whom I do not trust. For even if the heart is not fully resolved or well disposed, yet if there is any part of it that inclines to prayer, stick by it. It is a sure pledge that in that part of your heart, you believe.

[2] The *second* way to know whether faith is in you or not, is this: look within yourself and *see if your heart can be content to renounce your rancour, to forgive your grudges, and to do that freely for God's sake.* Can you do this? And will you forgive your neighbour as freely as God has forgiven you? Assuredly, this is a genuine effect of the Holy Spirit, for nature could never give it to you. There is nothing to which nature bends itself more than to rancour and envy, and there is nothing in which nature places her honour more greedily than in private revenge. Now if your heart is so tamed and humbled that it will willingly forgive the injury for God's sake, then that is a genuine effect of the Spirit. This is not my saying, but the saying of Christ Himself in the Gospel: 'if ye forgive men their trespasses, your heavenly Father will also forgive you; but if ye forgive not men their trespasses, neither will your Father forgive your trespasses' (Matt. 6:14 and 15). Thus Christ in effect says, He who forgives wrongs will have wrongs forgiven him, but he who revenges his own

wrongs, will have wrong revenged upon him. Therefore if you wish to be spared in your wrongs done to the Almighty God, do you spare your neighbour. I will not insist further. Examine whether you have faith or not; examine it by your desire to pray, and by the way you discharge your own private grudges. If you are lacking in these things, remember that a heart void of prayer and full of rancour is a heart that is faithless and meet for hell.

[3] The *third* effect of faith is *compassion*. You must bow your heart and extend your pity toward the poor members of Christ's Body, and do not suffer them to lack if you have plenty, for unless you have this compassion, you have no faith. Examine yourselves by these three effects, and if you find them at all, even in the smallest measure, you have genuine faith in your hearts, faith that is true and living. Assuredly, God will be merciful to you.

The great need for embattled faith to be nourished

Even though this faith of ours is lively, yet it is not perfect in this world, it requires continual augmentation, every day and every hour; it requires to be nourished constantly. The Apostles themselves prayed for this increase and said: 'Lord, increase our faith' (Luke 17:5). And our Master Himself commands us to pray for it. 'Lord, increase our faith. I believe; Lord, help my unbelief.' Christ's own command teaches us plainly that this faith needs to be continually nourished and helped. It cannot be helped, except by prayer, and therefore we ought always to continue in prayer. The terrible doubt, the strange pits of desperation, into which the dearest servants of God are cast, clearly teach that faith needs to be helped, and that we should be perpetually seeking in fear and trembling, to have it augmented. Yes indeed, the best servants of God are exercised with seasons of terrible doubt in their souls, with strange falterings, and they are brought at times, so it appears to them, to the very brink of desperation. These doubtings and falterings show us that this faith of ours requires to be perpetually nourished, and that we have need continually to pray for its increase. It pleases the Lord to let His servants see themselves at times in order to humble them, and show them how ugly sin is. It pleases Him to let them fall into the bitterness of sin, but not because He wishes to consume them, or suffer them to be swallowed up by desperation. For though Hezekiah cries out: 'As a lion, so will He break all my bones: from day to night wilt thou make an end of me' (Isa. 38:13), yet the Lord does not allow him to despair. And although David cries: 'How long, Lord? wilt thou be angry for ever? Shall thy jealousy burn like fire?' (Ps 79:5), yet he does not despair. The Lord casts His servants very low in order that they may feel in their hearts and consciences what Christ suffered for them in the Garden, and on the Cross, in Soul and Body. Indeed, we might be tempted to think that there has been plain collusion between the Father and the Son, and that His suffering was no suffering, unless we too felt in our souls something of the hell which He sustained in full measure on our behalf. So, in order that we may clearly understand the bitterness of sin, that we may know how far we are indebted to Christ, who suffered such torments for our sins, and that we may be more able to thank Him and praise His holy Name, He allows us, His own servants, to doubt, but not to despair. He forgives our doubtings, He forgives our falterings, and in His own time He supports us, and brings us to the waters of life.

These doubts, as I have often said, may lodge in a soul with faith, for doubt and faith are not directly opposed. Only faith and despair are directly opposed, and therefore faith and despair cannot both lodge in the same soul. Despair cuts away the pillars of hope, and where there is no hope, there can be no faith; but as for doubt, it may lodge, it will lodge, and has lodged, in the soul of the best servants that God ever had. Recall the words of the Apostle: 'We are perplexed [Geneva Bible, 'in doubt'] but not in despair' (2 Cor. 4:8). Thus doubt and faith may lodge both in one soul. Where does this doubting come from? We know that in the regenerate man there is a remnant of corruption, for we do not get our heaven on this earth. Although we begin our heaven here, we do not get it here completely. If all our corruption were taken away, what would remain but a complete heaven here? Thus it is only begun in this life, and not perfected, and so there is left in the soul a great corruption which is never idle, but is continually occupied. This corruption is ever giving birth to sin, sometimes more than at other times. Every sin hurts the conscience: a hurt conscience impairs the persuasion, and so doubt comes in. There is not a sin that we commit but it banishes light, and casts a slough over the eye of our faith, impairing our vision, so that we doubt and stumble. And were it not that the Lord in His mercy takes us up and gives us the gift of repentance, and makes us every day, as often as we sin, cry for mercy, and so repair the loss of our faith and of our feeling of mercy, we would continue in sin, and put out the light altogether. But it pleases the Lord, even if we sin every day, to give us the gift of repentance, and through repentance, to repair our faith, to repair the sense and feeling of mercy in us, and so to restore us to the same state of persuasion we were in before. Therefore if God does not begin, continue and end with mercy, in the very moment that He withdraws His mercy from us, we will decay, and so we must be diligent in calling upon His mercy. We must continually persist in seeking to have a feeling of mercy. So much, then, for the problem of doubt.

Though we may doubt, the gift of faith is never revoked

Now, however sure and certain it is that the faith of the best children of God is subject to doubt, it is just as sure and certain that doubt is never wholly extinct. Even if it is ever so weak, it will never decay and perish out of the heart entirely, once it makes residence in it. To sustain the troubled heart, the Spirit of God has set down this comfort and consolation in His Word, that however weak faith may be, nevertheless, a weak faith is faith, and that wherever faith is, there must be mercy. In Romans 11:29 we read: 'The gifts and calling of God are without repentance.' But among all His gifts of this kind, faith is one of the greatest; therefore it can never be revoked. In Jude verse 3 we read of 'the faith which was once delivered unto the saints'—'once delivered', that is, permanently given, never to be changed, nor utterly taken from them. The Lord will not repent of this gift, for the soul which He has once loved, He will love perpetually.

It is true and certain that the sparks of faith which are kindled in the heart by the Spirit of God, may be smothered for a long time, or covered up by the ashes of our own corruption, and by our own evil deeds and wickedness into which we fall. It is true that the effects of a living faith may be interrupted, and that lusts and wrong affections may prevail for a long time, so that when a man looks at himself in the light of the judgements of God that hang over soul and body, and when he looks at his dissolute life and at the anger of God against it, in the mind, heart and conscience of such a man, who has so smothered and oppressed his faith, there will often arise the conviction, as he fixes his eyes on himself alone, that he is a reprobate, an outcast, and will never be able to recover God's mercy. Where this corruption breaks out in such a gross way, after the Lord has called you, take care, as soon as the Lord begins to awaken you again, to fix your eyes at once upon your own life, and consider very seriously both the gravity of your sin, and the weight of the wrath of God which you see falling upon it. But if you stay fixed in these considerations, and are loth to permit your thoughts to dwell upon the depth of the mercy of God, then inevitably you come to feel in your own judgement that you are an outcast. And yet God forbid that it were so, for although these sparks of the Spirit are covered by the corruption within your soul, yet they are not wholly put out.

Let me show you that they are not extinguished. Even if they do not break forth in outward activity, so that the world may know you again as a faithful man, (1) nevertheless *these sparks are not idle*, and you will find that they are not idle in you. For confirmation of my argument, that they are not idle, even although our bodies are given over to excesses, after our effectual

calling within, think of a fire covered with ashes, for it is
still a fire. No one will say that the fire is put out,
although it is covered. No more is faith put out in the
soul, although it is so covered up that it does not appear
or show any light outwardly. We have a clear example of
this in David. After his lamentation in that Psalm of
repentance, he prays to God in these words: 'Cast me
not away from thy presence', and then adds 'And take
not thy Holy Spirit from me' (Ps 51:11). Had he not lost
the Spirit by his adultery and murder? No, for then he
would not have said, 'Take it not from me', but 'Restore
it to me'. It is true that he uses similar language in the
following verse, 'Restore unto me the joy of thy
salvation'. It is not that he lacked the Spirit wholly, but
that the Spirit lacked force in him, and needed strength-
ening and fortification. It needed to be stirred up, so
that its flame might appear. Therefore I say the fact that
David says so plainly after his adultery and murder,
'Take not thy Holy Spirit from me', is a certain argument
that the faithful never have the Spirit of God taken from
them, even in their greatest excesses.

(2) The second point is this. How do I prove that these
sparks are not idle, although the outward effects are
interrupted? As David felt this in his conscience, so
every one of you may feel it in your own conscience. The
Spirit of God in man's heart cannot be idle, for all the
time that the body is given over to dissoluteness, these
sparks of the Spirit keep accusing your dissoluteness,
and finding fault with your behaviour. They will not
allow you to enjoy the pleasures of your body, without
great bitterness and continual remorse. And dwelling
where they do, in the soul, they will make it echo their
cry sometime or other, at least once in twenty-four

hours: 'Alas, I am doing the evil which I would not, if I had power and strength to resist my lust. If I could be master of my desire, I would not do the evil that I do for all the world. If I had power to do the good that I would do, I would not leave it undone for all the world.' Thus, even though these sparks do not have sufficient force and strength at the moment to resist lust and prevent evil deeds, nevertheless they are perpetually at work in the heart, finding fault with your corruption, and refusing to let you indulge in your pleasure without pain. Then finally it forces you to give voice to such words as these: 'If I had strength to resist, I would not do the evil which I do.' Where there is a cry like this, it is unquestionably the cry of a soul which the Lord has begun to sanctify. And when once it is sanctified in spite of the devil and the corruption within, its faith will never perish.

However, if the whole soul, without any contradiction from within, but with a greedy appetite and pleasure, is carried away into evil, without any regret, then that soul is in an evil state. I can look for nothing for such a soul but death, unless the Lord prevents it. But where there is remorse and sorrow, and such a cry as this in the soul, it will recover strength in the time that God has appointed. The Lord will never allow these sparks to be wholly taken away, but in His own time He will kindle them, and make them break out before the world in good works. In His own time the Lord will sanctify them. He will scatter the ashes of corruption, stir up the sparks, and make them break out into a better life than ever they did before. Thus you may clearly see that David's repentance has done more good to the Church of God than if he had never fallen.

Even if the fruits of repentance are interrupted, yet the sparks are not extinguished. No man thinks that the fire which is covered with ashes is extinguished, for when it is stirred up in the morning, it will burn as brightly as it did the night before. No one will think that the trees are dead when in winter they are without leaves, fruit and external beauty. No one will think that the sun has gone out of the sky, although it is over-shadowed by a cloud of darkness and mist. There is a great difference between a sleepy disease, and death, for men are not dead if they are sleeping, and yet there is nothing more like death than sleep. As there is a great difference between a drunk man and a dead man, so there is a great difference between the faith that lies hid for a while, but does not express itself, and the light that is utterly put out. When we do not break forth into outward deeds, God forbid that we should think that these sparks are wholly extinguished. Indeed, the soul that is visited after foul defections from its calling and against its knowledge, before it recovers its former beauty, is in great danger. For if the Lord allows your corruption to have its way, so that it carries you where it will, and does everything it can to make you put out the sparks of regeneration, then when the Lord begins to challenge you, or make you render an account of your past life, your soul is in great danger.

Therefore, when the Lord begins to lay to your charge your dissolute life, the contempt and abuse of your calling, assuredly your soul is as near the brink of desperation as it could be. For if you look at God, you will see nothing but His anger, kindled like a fire against you. If you look at yourself, you will see nothing but sin provoking His anger, you will see the contempt and abuse of your calling increasing His anger; you will see nothing but matter for despair.

Our refuge in life's severest trials

What is the best pillar, and the surest refuge, on which such a soul, so near to the brink of desperation, may rely? I will show you a place of help in which, when you are assaulted by the severest trials, you may find repose. When there is nothing before you but death, when you see the devil accusing you, your own conscience bearing him witness against you, your life accusing you, and your abuse of your calling accusing you, where will you go? (1) *First*, look back over your past experience, turn over your memory, and *recall if God at any time has loved you at all*, if ever you have felt the love and favour of God in your heart and conscience. Remember, if ever the Lord has so disposed your heart, that as He loved you, you loved Him, and had a desire to obtain Him. Remember this, and rest your assurance on the fact, that as He loved you once, so He will love you always, and will assuredly restore you to that love before you die. The heart that has once felt this love of God will feel it again. The Lord will restore to His creatures before ever they depart from this life, the same gift or grace or taste of the powers of the world to come that He had already given them in this life. Therefore the soul that is tossed with severe assaults and great dangers where present experience will not help, must have recourse to the past, and keep in memory the former experience of mercy which the Lord has freely shown toward it. This same memory will be so pleasant to the soul that it will keep it from desperation in the present, and uphold it until the time when the Lord will pacify the heart, and give comfort to the soul. Then that soul will see that however angry God was, He was angry only for a little while.

I speak of these things, not because I think that every one of you has tasted them, and yet in some measure the servants of God must taste of them, while you who have not may yet taste of them before you die. And therefore, whether you have tasted them or not, it cannot but be profitable for you to lock up this lesson in your heart, and remember it faithfully, that if the Lord at any time should knock at your hearts, you may remember and say to yourselves: 'I learned how to look back to my past experience and find rest.' And although you yourselves are not put to it just now, yet when you visit those who are troubled in conscience, set these things before them as comforts, and use them as medicines most suited to apply to the grief of the inward conscience. Thus you will reap fruit from this doctrine and possess your souls in a good estate. That then is the first point in which every one of you ought to try and examine your own conscience.

[2] The *second* point is this: *see whether you have love toward your neighbour or not.* For as we have union with God by faith, so by the bond of love we have union with our neighbour; for love is the main branch that springs from the root of faith. Love is the celestial glue that joins together all the faithful members in the unity of the mystical Body. Religion was instituted by God to serve as a pathway to guide us to our chief felicity, and so we cannot be happy unless we are like our God; but unless we have love, we cannot be like Him. For as it says in 1 John 4:8, 'God is love'. Therefore, because God is love, he who would resemble Him must have love poured into him. This single

argument testifies to us that love is a principal end to which all things commanded in religion ought to be directed.

To spend long in the praise of love is not necessary, since the holy Scripture resounds in extolling it; but lest we speak ambiguously, I will explain to you how this word is used and understood in the Scriptures.

The Scripture's teaching on Love

Love is considered the spring and fountain from which all else proceeds, that is, the love whereby we love God. And as love comes first from God, and is poured by His Holy Spirit into our hearts, so (1) it first rebounds upwards and strikes back at God Himself, for the love of God always precedes the love of the creature. (2) Next, we use this word for the love whereby we love God's creatures, our neighbours, and especially those who are of the family of faith. (3) And thirdly, it is used for the deeds of the second Table of God's Law, which flow from this love. Now when I speak here of love, I use it in the second sense, namely, of the love of our neighbour. And this love I call 'the gift of God' poured into the hearts of men and women. It is by this gift that we first love God in Christ our Saviour; and then in God, and for God's sake, we love all His creatures, but chiefly our brethren, who are of the family of faith, the children who have one Father in common with us.

We will now examine this definition. (1) *First*, I say, *the love of God comes from God, and returns to God*; as it comes down from Him, so it strikes upward to Him again. Is there not good reason for saying that? Set the love of your heart as you will upon creatures, you will never be satisfied, nor will your affection ever be content, unless you lay hold upon God. But if once you love God in your heart, and cast your affection upon Him, and once you take hold of Him, the longer you love Him, the greater the satisfaction and contentment you will have. You will not thirst for any other. As for the creatures which God has created, every one of them is stamped with His own stamp, and every creature bears His image. When you contemplate the image of God in the creature, should it not draw you to Him, so that you do not fix your heart upon the creature itself? God's own image in His creature should lead you to Himself, therefore the more you know God's creatures, the greater the variety of your knowledge of them, the more should every detail in your knowledge of them draw you to God; and the more should you adore your God, and know your duty towards Him.

Moreover, since delight flows from knowledge, and every knowledge has its own delight, as the variety of knowledge that arises from God's creatures should make the mind mount up to the knowledge of God, so the variety of delights that arises from the diversity of this knowledge should move the heart upward to the love of God. When the heart gets hold of God, and is possessed with the love of God, and the mind is occupied with the true knowledge of God, then, as soon as the heart and mind are full of God, the heart is quiet, and the mind is satisfied. Therefore the more this knowledge grows in the mind, the greater the contentment you have; and the more the love of God grows in your heart, the greater the joy and rejoicing you have in your soul. Why? In God you have not only all the creatures, but you have Himself besides the creatures. And therefore in God you have all the knowledge and delight that can derive from the creatures; besides the creatures, you have God Himself, who is the Creator. And so, I say, the mind of man can never content itself in the knowledge, nor can the heart ever settle itself in the love, of mere creatures, for they are fleeting and vain, as Solomon calls them; but in the infinite God, rightly known and earnestly loved, the mind will find complete rest, and the heart will have perfect joy. Our affection is so insatiable that no finite being will ever satisfy it, nor can there be any permanent contentment with the thing that is transitory. Thus love ought to mount upward and redound first toward God, in whose face the heart will find full and perfect joy.

(2) The *second* argument that I use is as follows: There is only one precept left by our Master which we are commanded to obey, namely, that *every one of us should love one another*. Understanding well that where love was, there was no need for more laws, and that by love alone the life of man should be most happy, our wise Master left us only this one principal Commandment, which sums up the whole Law and the Gospel in one word: 'Love'. And if the heart of man is filled with love, his life will be most happy and blessed, for there is nothing that makes this life happy except the resemblance and likeness that we have with God. The nearer we draw to God, the more blessed is our life, for there cannot be a life so happy as the life of God. Now, says St John, in his First Epistle, 'God is love' (4:8); therefore the more we draw near to love, the nearer we are to that happy life, for then we are in God, and are partakers of the life of God.

When I speak thus, you must not think that love in God and love in us is one thing; for love is but a quality

213

in us, but it is not a quality in God. There is nothing in God but what God Himself is, and so love in God is His own essence. Therefore, the more you grow in love, the nearer you draw to God, and to that happy and blessed life. There is nothing more profitable, more agreeable, and congruous to nature, than to love, and above all things, to love God. That is why God and His angels are most happy and blessed, because they love all things, and desire ever to do good. On the other hand, there is nothing more unhappy, nothing more harmful, more hurtful, and that destroys nature more, than to burn with envy and hatred. Hence it is that the devils are most miserable, who torment themselves with continual malice and hatred, burning with a vehement appetite to be harmful to all creatures. As the life of the devil is most unhappy, because he is full of envy and malice, so our life must be most happy, if we are full of love. I will speak no more of it, except to say: if you have love, note the fruits of love as they are set down in 1 Corinthians 13:4, 5, 6, 7. If you do not have these in some measure, then you do not have true love.

I end here. You see in what points every one of you ought to be prepared: you must be endowed with this love, and with faith, and if you have these in any small degree, go forward boldly to hear the Word, and to receive the Sacrament. This is the preparation that we allow. I grant that the Papists have a preparation very different from this, but they can have no warrant for it from the Word of God. Last of all, since we are commanded to examine ourselves, he who lacks knowledge cannot examine himself. A mad man cannot examine himself. A child cannot examine himself—therefore they ought not to come to the Lord's Table. When due account has been taken of all these things, he who has faith and love in any measure at all, ought to come to the Table. And this applies equally to the hearing of the Word, and to the receiving of the Sacrament. Therefore, may the Lord in His mercy enlighten your minds, and work some measure of faith and love in your hearts, that you may be partakers of that heavenly life offered in the Word and Sacraments, that you may begin your heaven here, and obtain its full fruition in the life to come, through the righteous merits of Christ Jesus. To whom with the Father and the Holy Ghost be all honour, praise and glory, now and for ever. Amen.

Christian Focus Publications

publishes books for all ages

Our mission statement –

STAYING FAITHFUL

In dependence upon God we seek to help make His infallible Word, the Bible, relevant. Our aim is to ensure that the Lord Jesus Christ is presented as the only hope to obtain forgiveness of sin, live a useful life and look forward to heaven with Him.

REACHING OUT

Christ's last command requires us to reach out to our world with His gospel. We seek to help fulfill that by publishing books that point people towards Jesus and help them develop a Christ-like maturity. We aim to equip all levels of readers for life, work, ministry and mission.

Books in our adult range are published in three imprints.

Christian Focus contains popular works including biographies, commentaries, basic doctrine and Christian living. Our children's books are also published in this imprint.

Mentor focuses on books written at a level suitable for Bible College and seminary students, pastors, and other serious readers. The imprint includes commentaries, doctrinal studies, examination of current issues and church history.

Christian Heritage contains classic writings from the past.

Christian Focus Publications, Ltd
Geanies House, Fearn,
Ross-shire, IV20 1TW, Scotland, United Kingdom
info@christianfocus.com

www.christianfocus.com